IMAGES OF ENGLAND

# TAVISTOCK
## REVISITED

IMAGES OF ENGLAND

# TAVISTOCK
## REVISITED

GERRY WOODCOCK

*Frontispiece*: This beautiful building, the Brook Street Congregational church, was for almost a century a well-loved town centre landmark. Opened in 1873, it was demolished in 1964 and was replaced by the Pearl Assurance Co. office block (see page 22).

First published in 2005 by Tempus Publishing

Reprinted in 2010 by
The History Press
The Mill, Brimscombe Port,
Stroud, Gloucestershire, GL5 2QG
www.thehistorypress.co.uk

British Library Cataloguing in Publication Data.
A catalogue record for this book is available from the British Library.

ISBN 978 0 7524 3711 8

Typesetting and origination by Tempus Publishing.
Printed in Great Britain.

# Contents

Tavistock Goosey Vair

by

C. John Trythall


Tiz jist a month come Vriday nex'
Bill Camperdown an' me
Us draiv'd acrass aul Dartymoor
Th' Goozey Vair t'zee
Us maade ourzel's quate viddy
Us shaved an' graized our ayer
Then off us gaws een our Zindy Claws
Be'ind Bill's aul grey mare.
Us smilled th' zage an' onions
Aul th' way vrom Whitchurch Down
An' did'n us 'av a blaw out
When us put up een town
An' there us met Ned 'Annaford
Jan Stewer an' Nicky Square
An' it zimmed to me aul Dem mus' be
T' Tavistock GoozeyVair.

*Chorus:*
*An' it's aul an' wer be gwain?*
*An' what be doin' ov ther'?*
*'Aive down yer prong*
*An' step down 'long*
*T' Tavistock Goozey Vair*


Tavistock's own anthem celebrates its annual fair. This is the first verse and
chorus.

# Introduction

This is a sequel to the book on Tavistock that I compiled in 1997 for the Archive Photographs Series. The format and general approach remain the same but the content is completely different. This is a fresh compilation of pictures, some of them taking a new look at familiar settings and situations and others reflecting more unusual places and happenings. The focus remains firmly on the town and the community that belongs to it. Tavistock has cast a spell over generations of visitors. One of the clues to this can be found in its setting. It lies between two significant natural barriers. To the west is the Tamar Valley, beyond which is Cornwall with its distinctive characteristics and history. To the east, the expanse of Dartmoor separates the town in much more than a physical sense from other parts of Devon. Residents and visitors might still recognise the truth of the words of an impressed tourist who observed in 1892 that 'the town has a leisurely and beautiful appearance, and the people do not seem to need to kill themselves and slay each other in the mad rush of life which spoils so many other towns'. But being relaxed is not the same as being sleepy. The economic and social life of the town has, at each stage of its development, been dynamic. The visitor who sees the designation 'Ancient Stannary Town' on the roadside welcoming-plate is immediately reminded of the long association with the tin industry. Similarly the oft-quoted description, the 'Gothic Town of the West', brings to mind the great age of copper-mining, the profits from which helped to pay for the Victorian redevelopment of the town centre. In one sense, Tavistock, nestling comfortably in the valley of the Tavy, has been insulated from some of the pressures that have brought about change in other places. This has given a certain distinctiveness to its development. On the other hand, the problems, the tensions, the achievements, the disasters and the victories that have punctuated the lives of other communities have all been part of the Tavistock experience. The fundamental fact is that history forges a community on the anvil of shared experience. Tavistock, on this definition, is certainly a community.

This book, and others like it, leans heavily on the work of the camera. Photography is, however, a new art and science. There are no images of Tavistock through the lens before the middle of the nineteenth century. The camera was not present to record most of the great events in the 1,000-year period of the community's recorded history, or to provide a commentary on the daily lives of its members. If we want to know more about the influence of the great Benedictine abbey, founded in 974, in the shadow of which the medieval town passed from infancy to adolescence, we must turn not to photographs but to documents and to the work of artists and chroniclers. The same is true of the long period that followed the dissolution of the monasteries in 1539, when for four centuries a relationship existed between the town and the dynasty that provided it with a line of patrons in the form of successive Earls, later Dukes, of Bedford. Fortunately the marks made by these two long epochs on the development of Tavistock have proved to be both substantial and indelible. But if only a photographer had been lurking when the Danes sacked the place in 997, or when the monks were driven from their abbey in 1539, or when Charles I made his visit in 1644, or when the first ball was bowled at the cricket club's home, The Ring, in 1849, or when the hustings collapsed during a by-election meeting in 1857, or...

Photography has added a new dimension to historical enquiry. It is a tool that helps us to explain what we were, and thereby helps us to understand what we are. In Tavistock, the pioneers from the 1850s on were talented amateurs like town librarian William Merrifield and, of a later generation, Henry Creber. By the turn of the century, the age of the professional had arrived, with Samuel Gimblett in business in Market Street, Arthur Holden in King Street, Stanley Wadge in Brook Street and the Pearce brothers in West Street. In the first quarter of the new century came the golden age of the postcard, followed by an explosion in press and publicity photography. Examples from these, and other sources, form the backbone of this book.

The first, and longest, chapter of the book, 'The Setting', is an attempt to give an impression of the physical appearance of the town in its historical setting – vistas, open spaces, roads, streets, squares, waterways and buildings. In the other eight chapters, the emphasis is sharply on the people and their doings. In compiling the pictures, I have leaned on the Tavistock Local History Society's photographic archive housed in the town museum. This includes the holdings associated with William Merrifield and Eric Kingdon, the volumes of postcards presented in memory of Patience Duckham and, most significantly, the Thorington collection, kindly donated to the museum by Shirley Thorington as a memorial to her late husband Jim, the well-remembered professional photographer. In thanking Shirley, I would like also to acknowledge the help of Jim's old paper, the *Tavistock Times Gazette*, and his successor, James Bird. Institutions to which I am grateful include the Subscription Library, Tavistock College, Kelly College and The Wharf arts centre. My thanks also go to Chris Aggett, Moira Andrews, Phil Creber, Robert Edwards, Marjorie Greening, Graham Kirkpatrick, Rod Martin, Robin Pike, Paul Rendell, Tony Smith, Muriel Tucker and Gerald Wasley. I have done my best to check the accuracy of names, places and dates but I willingly accept responsibility for any errors that have survived this scrutiny. The book is dedicated to my fellow Tavistockians past and present, whose doings are recorded in its pages.

Gerry Woodcock
*September 2005*

one

# The Setting

For many visitors to Tavistock over the years, the first view of the town was from the London and South Western Railway station. Looking south from the adjacent viaduct, such landmarks as the parish church and the Town Hall feature clearly. The spot can be revisited today because the viaduct forms part of a public walkway.

A 1970 view from the same direction, spanning the town centre from Vigo Bridge on the left to the Bedford Hotel on the right. Dolvin Road and its trees provide a backcloth, while the foreground shows the parallel routes of Drake Road, Bannawell Street, and Glanville Road, the former two emerging from the shadow of the recently redundant viaduct.

A view from above Mount Tavy Road, looking northwards across Parkwood. Taken in the mid-twentieth century, it shows the Tavy, the GWR railway line and Okehampton Road, all converging on the town from the east. Residential Parkwood lies between the riverside industrial buildings in the foreground and Kelly College in the distance.

The western part of the town in 1927, pictured from the church tower. Prominent are the two Methodist chapels and Fitzford church beyond, with West Street standing out clearly as the important artery that it was.

Francis Drake, Tavistock's most famous son, was born at Crowndale. The building has not survived. This sketch was made in the nineteenth century on the evidence of eyewitness accounts of its state at that time.

West Street in the 1870s. It is perhaps a Sunday lunchtime, as the street is quiet. A little knot of people have gathered round a cart outside Mrs Jane Ridgway's haberdashery, just above the Cornish Arms. Cox Tor smiles down on a town taking a midday nap.

The camera, mounted in the Old Mine Field above Plymouth Road, is pointed north-west to take in the toll-house guarding the Tudor West Bridge and, beyond, Fitzford. The year is 1910. Cows graze where, a century later, primary-school children will learn and play. Beyond are Fitzford church, the Duke's cottages and the restored gatehouse.

Standing by Callington Road and looking eastward provides not only a panorama of the town but also views of Whitchurch Down and Dartmoor beyond. The foreground is dominated by the Victorian church, built by the Duke of Bedford to provide for the growing population of miners. It now serves the Roman Catholic community. The original gasworks nestle below.

Two changes to the Fitzford landscape occurred in the 1860s, with the building of the church and the demolition of the gatehouse. The latter was the only remaining part of the medieval Fitzford Mansion. This picture, dated 1869, confirms that both operations were going on at the same time. Two years later, the gatehouse was reconstructed on the same site.

In 1859, Parliament passed the Tavistock Market Act, which gave the Duke of Bedford the green light to carry through a major programme of town centre redevelopment. The result was the emergence, in the early 1860s, of the Pannier Market and the new Duke Street, and, almost as an afterthought since it was not specifically mentioned in the Act, the Town Hall. This is the Town Hall as it appeared in 1880.

From the vantage point of Abbey Bridge, the camera takes us through Abbey Place into Bedford Square in 1880. On the northern side of the square is the old *The Tavistock Gazette* building, under the end of which is a covered passage leading to an alley where the original post office was situated.

A similar view, this time in 1906. The quarter of a century between the two pictures has produced a major development. Post Office Lane and its accompanying buildings have disappeared, to be replaced by Drake Road, which was driven through and built up to provide suitable access to the new LSWR station that has appeared above, on Kilworthy Hill.

The Tavy is a river of moods. Here, in the 1870s, it shows itself calm, inviting and benign in a period of dry weather. The background is the familiar Abbey Bridge, which had been recently widened and partially rebuilt to cope with the traffic to the new GWR station on the left bank of the river. The weir was to be destroyed in the flood of 1890.

The river is fed by innumerable Dartmoor streams and when it has eaten too heartily it shows symptoms of irritable indigestion and throws tantrums, as occurred here in the 1970s. Also featured here are the wall marking the limit of the abbey precinct, the point close to the weir from which water is taken to feed the Tavistock Canal, and the premises of the West Devon Club, opened in 1899.

In 1822, a new road was constructed to replace the old road from Tavistock to Plymouth, via Whitchurch. The new route exited the town over West Bridge and has remained the main road ever since. In the nineteenth century, there was some uncertainty about the name to be given to the town stretch of the new thoroughfare, and maps normally referred to it as New Road. The twentieth century finally settled on Plymouth Road. The Bedford estate office and the Bedford Hotel are featured here.

Edward Bray, son of the Duke's steward, was born in Abbey House, which later became the Bedford Hotel, in 1778. In 1812, he became vicar of Tavistock and held the living until his death in 1857. He was the first occupant of the new vicarage, built alongside his birthplace. Nearly two centuries and ten incumbents later, it remains the vicarage.

Between 974 and 1539, the greatest influence on the lives of the people of Tavistock was the great Benedictine house, the Abbey of Our Lady and St Rumon. Little of it survives, its position having made its buildings an easy prey after the dissolution of the monasteries. An exception is the riverside two-storey Still Tower, in which the monks distilled their potions and prepared their pick-me-ups. It still guards the southern corner of the monastic precinct.

A few paces from the Still Tower is Betsy Grimbal's Tower, glowering sombrely at the vicarage in front and scowling disapprovingly at the revellers in the Bedford Hotel behind. There is a myth that this marks the spot where a lady named Betsy Grimbal was murdered, presumably by a deranged monk. However, we are on much safer ground in supposing that this, one of the four entrances into the abbey precinct, was named in honour of the Blessed Grimbald, a ninth-century saint.

Four road bridges cross the Tavy as it flows through the town. The highest, and newest, is Stannary Bridge, which was built in 1995. Vigo Bridge and Abbey Bridge were eighteenth-century constructions to carry turnpike roads out to Moretonhampstead and Plymouth respectively. West Bridge was built in the middle of the sixteenth century to replace a ford. The earliest bridge was medieval and occupied a position midway between the present Abbey and Vigo Bridges; it was demolished in the eighteenth century. This is a drawing of it by T.R. Crabtree, after a detail in Charles Delafontaine's print of 1741.

An Edwardian scene captured by a photographer standing opposite the cemetery gates. The river Tavy is on the left and Plymouth Road on the right. Between the two are West Bridge Cottages, built by the Duke of Bedford in the middle of the nineteenth century.

*Above:* In the first half of the nineteenth century, the Canal Wharf was one of the busiest places in Tavistock. This was where cargoes, principally of copper ore, were loaded onto barges for transportation along the 4½ mile route to the Tamarside port of Morwellham. In 1873, competition from the railway led to the canal's redundancy. The waterway, and the accompanying warehouse buildings, fell into disuse. Some of the latter were rescued and given another function, but the tone of the wharf area became little more than a whispering echo of former days.

*Below:* The opening of an arts centre in 1995 brought to life a daring and visionary project. The accommodation was a group of canalside warehouse buildings that had for some years been used as a coal depot and storage shed. The new premises offered facilities for theatre, film, concerts and a wide range of arts activities.

Market Street, 1914. As the name implies, this was the commercial heart of the community from the earliest times. Neighbours on the east side of the road are Eastmans Ltd butchers and the confectionery shop of Mrs Elizabeth Cole, who also ran a restaurant round the corner in Bedford Square. Market Street also housed at that time two hairdressers, two bootmakers, two grocers, two banks, a milliner, a baker, a saddler, a painter, an outfitter, another butcher and the Co-op.

An early twentieth-century view of Bannawell Street from the foot of Madge Lane. Always one of the town's most populous roads, Bannawell Street at that time accommodated 100 families in its seventy-eight dwellings. The workhouse and a chapel were also situated in this street, and two insurance agents and two dairymen ran businesses here. A boy can be seen standing outside No. 4, where James Acton made boots.

This was Duke Street after the Congregational church was demolished in 1964 (see page 2).

The Pearl Assurance Co. office block replaced the church.

*Opposite above:* Brook Street in 1906, at which time it housed forty-two businesses. Until the twentieth century, the population of Tavistock was concentrated almost exclusively on the north bank of the river, spreading out on either side of a road that ran east-west from Parkwood to Fitzford. This artery began modestly as Brook Street, assumed some grandeur as Duke Street and ended in West Street with a gentle climb towards Ford Street and a western exit.

*Opposite below:* The western end of Brook Street in the 1950s. The White Hart Hotel, long associated with the name of Stanley Goode who was proprietor for many years, was coming to the end of a century-long life. It had been the favourite haunt of American troops stationed here during the Second World War. Hoare's hairdressing business had been established in the street since the 1920s. In between sits an estate agent's, then a less common feature of the town centre landscape than in later years.

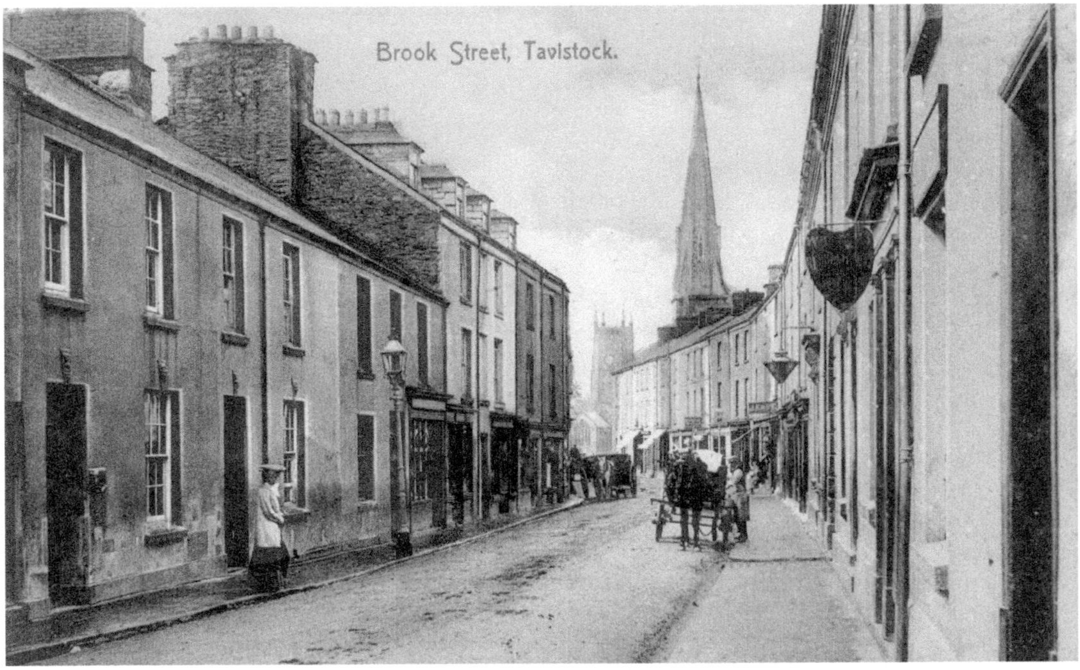
Brook Street, Tavistock.

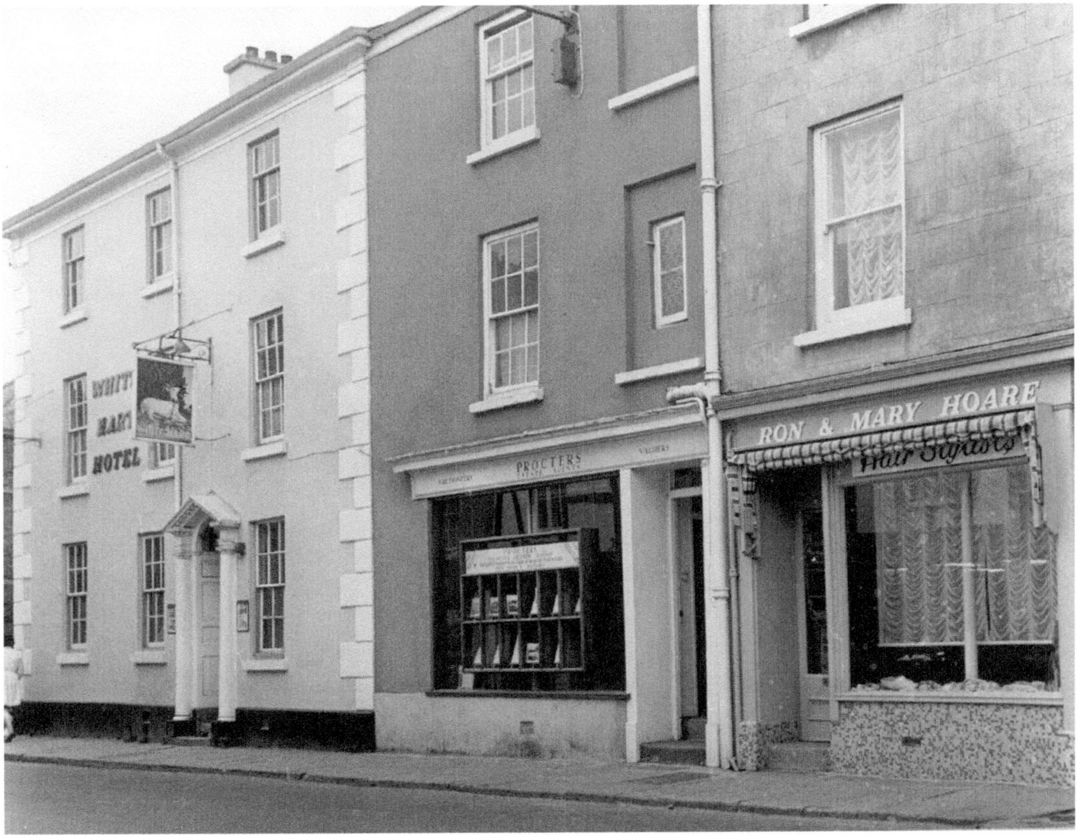
HOTEL
PROCTERS
RON & MARY HOARE

Tavistock's first hospital, opened in 1887, was a small building at the foot of Spring Hill. Nine years later, it was replaced by a new building further up the hill. This picture was taken in 1932.

The post office, seen here on the right, moved in 1859 from cramped premises in Post Office Lane to a building close to Abbey Bridge. It has remained there ever since, surviving a series of improvements and modifications. This photograph was taken by William Merrifield, presumably from a first-floor window in his Guildhall Square cottage.

In 1911, the eleventh Duke of Bedford offered the majority of his Tavistock properties for sale. Among the assets acquired by the town council was a large open space between the Tavy and Plymouth Road traditionally known as The Meadows. The council provided amenities such as a paddling pool and redesignated it the Pleasure Grounds. The people sensibly stuck with The Meadows.

THE OUTLOOK. DARTMOOR.

Another open space that, along with The Meadows, occupies a special place in the affections of Tavistockians is Whitchurch Down. Close to the Golf House stands the Pimple, built by the distinguished architect Sir Edwin Lutyens in 1914. It is a beautiful folly, constructed for a limited function as a cover for a reservoir serving Littlecourt and, later, other Down Road residences. The photographer has conjured an atmospheric feeling for his postcard picture.

The West Street photographer T.E. Pearce took this picture of Mount Tavy House in 1911, at an occasion to mark the Coronation of George V. Built in 1800, the house was the home of the Carpenter family until 1886. It has, since 1940, accommodated Mount House School.

Another T.E. Pearce photograph, this one of The Priory in 1900. The house was originally a farmhouse known as Tiddybrook. It was substantially rebuilt in the nineteenth century, incorporating a medieval entrance tower from the earlier structure. The Priory is a complete misnomer, echoing a fanciful legend that the building was actually once a priory. The house has been, in recent years, alternately a private house and a school.

Grenofen Manor in 1910, not yet shorn of its ivy covering. The Pearces were prolific photographers for commercial purposes and this is one of Sydney's less well-known pictures of local houses. The origins of Grenofen Manor lie in the eighteenth century but the century-long association with the Chichester family began in 1853. The property was converted into a number of residential apartments in 1997.

Holwell, the 'place of the holy well', was the site of a medieval mansion which was for more than three centuries the seat of the Glanville family. Virtually rebuilt in the nineteenth century, it was for a time the residence of John Taylor, the engineer whose legacy was the Tavistock Canal. It has remained a secluded private residence.

# HONOUR OAK TREE

MARKED BOUNDARY OF FRENCH PRISONERS ON PAROLE
IN TAVISTOCK FROM PRINCETOWN
DURING THE NAPOLEONIC WAR (1803 - 14).
ALSO WHERE MONEY WAS DEPOSITED
IN EXCHANGE FOR FOOD
DURING A CHOLERA OUTBREAK IN 1832.

*Above:* On the Tavistock to Whitchurch road, and marking a traditional boundary between the two parishes, is an oak tree. During the Napoleonic War, many captured enemy officers were confined in towns like Tavistock, where they were put on their honour not to stray beyond the boundary.

*Left:* The colonisation of Dolvin Road began, in 1834, with the dead. The living followed, on the other side of the road. Between 1845 and 1848, the Bedford estate built eighteen cottages, the prototypes for a further 250 that were to appear on various local sites over the next twenty years. This is No. 20 Dolvin Road, a house which is interesting not only because it displays the initial of its benefactor and the year of its construction but also because it was the birthplace of William Crossman, who was knighted during his term as Lord Mayor of Cardiff.

*Above:* Whitchurch Road, 1904. This was the original turnpike road out towards Plymouth but had long been superseded. As a thoroughfare, it had become secluded and rather neglected. The old road had to await the arrival of the motor car before it regained the noise and bustle of a busy artery. This is the stretch between The Priory and Hunson Villa.

*Below:* Whitchurch, although now part of the parish of Tavistock, retains many of the physical characteristics of village life. The Whitchurch Inn, viewed here in the late nineteenth century, has medieval origins. In its long history in the ownership of the Church, it has offered both hospitality to travellers and pilgrims and also been the focus for many local events.

Whitchurch Road, 1902. The camera points north-west to pick out the road, which is not yet bounded by housing estates, and, to the left, the GWR line on an embankment between Anderton and Whitchurch Halt.

Another early nineteenth-century view of Whitchurch. In the foreground, the road climbs steeply on its way to Grenofen. Looking north, the line of houses on Church Hill takes the eye to the tower of St Andrew's church and to the school on the opposite side of the road.

two

# Caring and Sharing

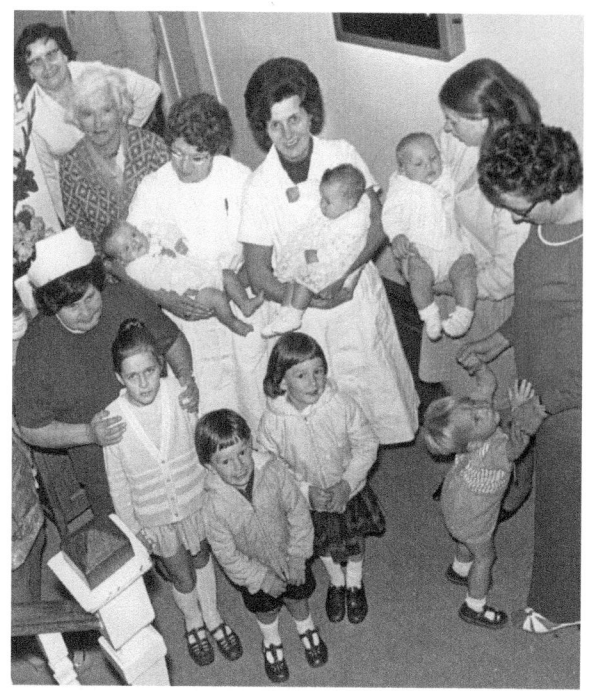

*Left:* The Tavistock Maternity Home opened on Whitchurch Road in 1953, after Dr Freddy Watt had argued in 1945 that 'facilities should be available in Tavistock for women to be confined where home confinement is not suitable'. At 8.15 p.m. on 6 May 1953, Mrs Gedge of Drake Gardens gave birth to the first child to be born there. The home survived a number of threats over the years but was finally closed in 1995.

*Below:* The newly formed Tavistock playgroup gets stuck into a practical session, with some adult supervision, in March 1967. The venue is the Youth Centre, a building that occupied a site next to the Methodist chapel between 1967 and 1993. The birth of the playgroup movement was a phenomenon of the 1960s.

*Above:* The birth of the Scouting movement nationally in 1908 was followed in 1909 by the establishment of the first Tavistock group. Some local troops of Scouts and Guides developed under the wing of particular churches or schools. The board in front of this group, for example, reads '2nd Tavistock Dolvin Road School'. The site is the school, the period is the 1920s, and the gentleman in the trilby is the headmaster, A.B. Treloar.

*Below:* Teenagers Helena O'Connor and Simon Cowderoy lead a music session during Playweek. In the 1970s a group of parents, anxious to offer young children a week of positive activities in the middle of the long summer holiday, organised programmes of indoor and outdoor events, and Playweek established itself as a regular mid-August feature.

Parents and children at a children's party in the Whitchurch Parish Room, Christmas 1947.

When the old *The Tavistock Gazette* folded in 1974, its stately offices were converted for community use and renamed Kingdon House. The Community Association that ran the new venture held a series of fundraising events, including an ox roast. Advertising the event in July 1977 are some of the Association's supporters. From left to right: Dinah Woodcock, Joanne Thompson, Mark Woodcock, Simon Edwards, Meg Parker, Graham Udle and Norna Beadle.

Molly Owen, the mother of the politician David Owen, was a tenacious campaigner on behalf of the handicapped, and it was largely through her efforts that the centre that bears her name was established in Tavistock. It serves a dual purpose as a social centre and a training agency. This was the 1970 Christmas Party.

The St John Ambulance organisation has been active in Tavistock since 1880, when a local brigade was formed. A century on and the brigade was continuing to attract the loyalty of a considerable number of young people, as this 1975 picture indicates.

Pupils from the county primary school wait outside their school in Plymouth Road to board a bus for a trip to London in the mid-1970s.

Another outing, in the same period. Looking forward to a break in Bournemouth in May 1974 are old-age pensioners, who have gathered, sensibly dressed, at the bus station.

*Opposite below:* On 9 August 2001, the new library was opened on a site between Plymouth Road and The Wharf. Doing the honours were the Marquis and Marchioness of Tavistock, pictured here with West Devon mayor Robin Pike and his wife Diana. The Marquis became the fourteenth Duke of Bedford in 2002 but sadly died in the following year.

The first public library in the town was opened in 1799 in the upper storey of a Market Street bookshop. In 1822, it gained a new home in a classically designed edifice built in Bedford Square, of which this is an artist's impression. The building was criticised for being out of keeping with surrounding styles and for obstructing the potential development of the area. It was demolished in 1831 and the library retreated to Court Gate.

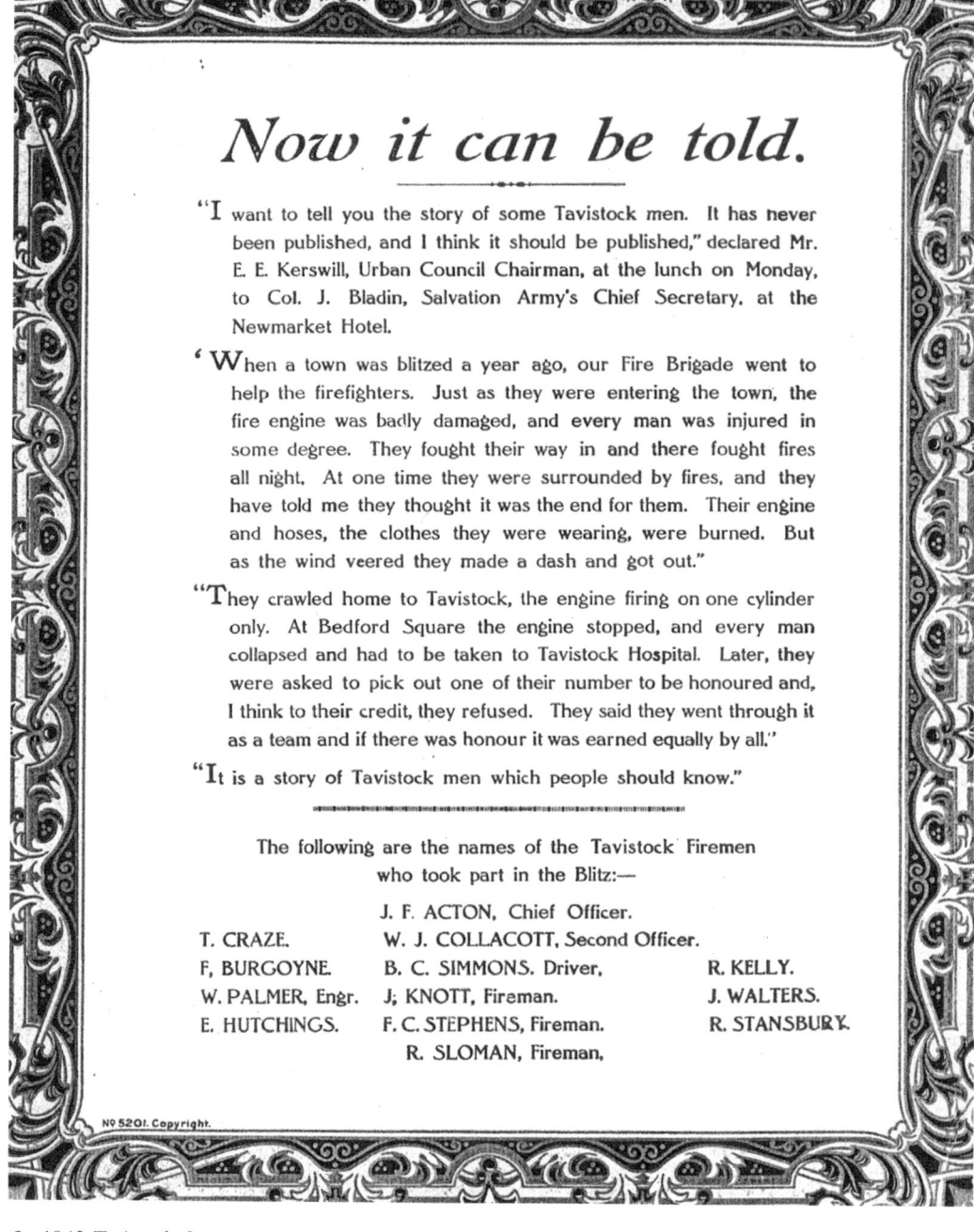

# Now it can be told.

"I want to tell you the story of some Tavistock men. It has never been published, and I think it should be published," declared Mr. E. E. Kerswill, Urban Council Chairman, at the lunch on Monday, to Col. J. Bladin, Salvation Army's Chief Secretary, at the Newmarket Hotel.

'When a town was blitzed a year ago, our Fire Brigade went to help the firefighters. Just as they were entering the town, the fire engine was badly damaged, and every man was injured in some degree. They fought their way in and there fought fires all night. At one time they were surrounded by fires, and they have told me they thought it was the end for them. Their engine and hoses, the clothes they were wearing, were burned. But as the wind veered they made a dash and got out."

"They crawled home to Tavistock, the engine firing on one cylinder only. At Bedford Square the engine stopped, and every man collapsed and had to be taken to Tavistock Hospital. Later, they were asked to pick out one of their number to be honoured and, I think to their credit, they refused. They said they went through it as a team and if there was honour it was earned equally by all."

"It is a story of Tavistock men which people should know."

The following are the names of the Tavistock Firemen who took part in the Blitz:—

J. F. ACTON, Chief Officer.
T. CRAZE.      W. J. COLLACOTT, Second Officer.
F, BURGOYNE.      B. C. SIMMONS. Driver,      R. KELLY.
W. PALMER, Engr.      J; KNOTT, Fireman.      J. WALTERS.
E. HUTCHINGS.      F. C. STEPHENS, Fireman.      R. STANSBURY.
R. SLOMAN, Fireman,

Nº 5201. Copyright.

In 1942, Tavistock firemen were honoured for their bravery during the 1941 bombing raids. The town referred to is Plymouth.

*Opposite below:* TAMEDS (Tamar Emergency Doctors Scheme) was formed to provide an emergency medical service in the area. Fundraising was undertaken to acquire essential equipment, in particular a defibrillator. Angela Rippon, flanked by Steve Grummitt and Dr Brian Steggles, draws a winning ticket in a raffle, watched by other local supporters.

The fire brigade in the 1970s, in their Market Road headquarters. The chief, John Philpott, with his white helmet, takes centre stage. From left to right, back row: Reg Craze, Mike Walters, Maurice Woods, Cliff Hocking, Fred Phillips, Graham Jackman. Front row: Mike Felles, Mr Worrell, Mr Stone, Bernard Chamings, Les Spencer, Chris Neale, Phil Creber.

The Union Workhouse, serving the local parishes, operated from rather forbidding premises at the top of Bannawell Street from 1838 to 1961. It is shown here in the early years of the twentieth century.

The Townswomen's Guild is an organisation whose main interests are defined as civics, homecraft, handicraft and the arts. In Tavistock, a Guild was formed in 1934. Members formed a choir, seen here in the 1950s rehearsing before an event in the church hall. The Guild closed some three years ago.

In its first year, 1987, the Local History Society mounted an exhibition in the Town Hall. A group of founder members were persuaded to clutch interesting items from the display as they posed for the camera. From left to right: Robin Fenner, Pat Murray, Alex Mettler, Joyce Metcalfe, Wynn Scutt, Joy Beer, Robin Pike, Gerry Woodcock, Margaret Heath, –?–, Sue Davies, John Davies.

A group almost as exotic as the one above. But what are these ladies up to? The known facts are that the picture was taken on 5 May 1896 at No. 3 Abbey Mead. It was sent to a friend, Emily Chegwyn, by Mrs Swale, who, with her husband, Dr Harold Swale, had lived at that address for some eighteen years before moving away when Dr Swale retired in May 1896.

*Above:* Wild nights at the Town Hall 1: Jim Ball tries single-handedly to keep order as old age pensioners enthusiastically accept Rotary Club largesse.

*Below:* Wild nights at the Town Hall 2: Members of the Wine Circle make merry.

*Above:* Doings on the Down 1: Whitchurch Down has been, over the years, the setting for a wide range of celebrations and events. In the early years of the twentieth century, it provided a popular venue for a number of youth organisations which included summer camps in their programmes. Among them were cadets, Scouts, church groups and, as this 1909 postcard shows, the YMCA.

*Right:* Doings on the Down 2: One of the most unusual episodes in the history of Whitchurch Down occurred in 1973. The Plaster Down camp, which was built during the Second World War to house an American military hospital, was on the point of closure and demolition. The sudden arrival of a large number of Ugandan Asians, who were seeking asylum after having been thrown out of their own country without belongings, changed the picture, as the camp was required to perform one final duty and provide transit camp facilities for these refugees. The local community was very generous in supplying emergency requirements.

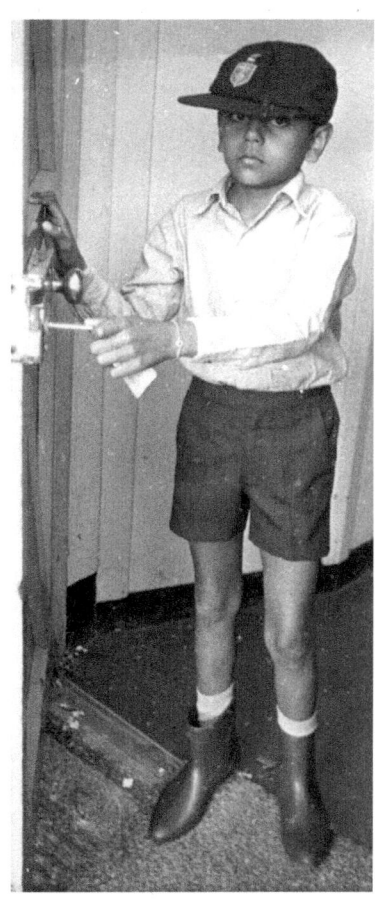

The Dartmoor Rescue Group was established in 1969, with Tavistock as one of its four moorside bases. Pioneer members of the Tavistock group discuss the question of liaison with the police with PC Jack Lamerton.

In 1970, local teachers celebrated the centenary of the 1870 Education Act and of the National Union of Teachers. At a centenary dinner in the Town Hall, the guest of honour was the NUT's General Secretary, Sir Edward Britton, seen here on the left. On the right is Ken Saxby, president of the Tavistock Association of the NUT. Between them, from left to right, are Mrs Saxby, Mrs Millward, John Poxon, Thelma Wood and Hayden Millward.

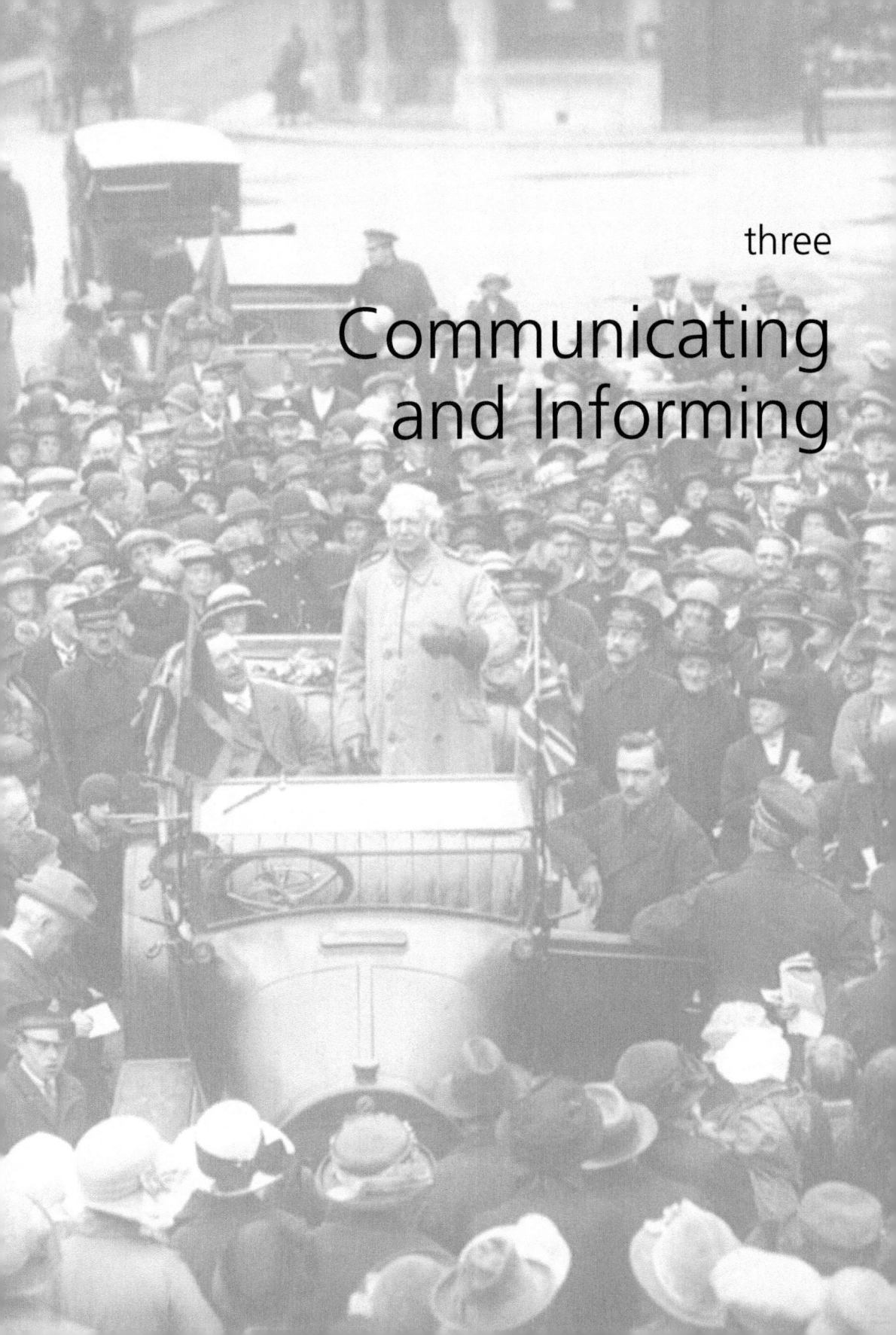

three

# Communicating
# and Informing

# The Tavistock Gazette
## AND WEEKLY ADVERTISER.
PUBLISHED BY GEORGE SPENCER, HIGHER MARKET STREET, TAVISTOCK, EVERY FRIDAY.

No. 1.　　　　　FRIDAY, SEPTEMBER 4, 1857.　　　　　PRICE ONE PENNY

# The Tavistock Gazette,
## AND WEEKLY ADVERTISER FOR DEVON AND CORNWALL.

Circulating in Beerferris, Brentor, Bickleigh, Bridestowe, Buckland, Calstock, Coryton, Chillaton, Gunnislake, Horrabridge, Kelly, Lydford, Lifton, Lewdown, Lamerton, Milton Abbot, Morwellham, Marytavy, Meavy, Princetown, Petertavy, Stokeclimsland, Sydenham, Walkhampton, Whitchurch.
PUBLISHED EVERY FRIDAY, BY T. W. GREENFIELD, BEDFORD SQUARE, TAVISTOCK, FOR THE TAVISTOCK PRINTING COMPANY, LIMITED.

REGISTERED FOR TRANSMISSION IN THE UNITED KINGDOM AND ABROAD]　　　　　[Free by Post 2s. per Quarter, or anywhere out of the United Kingdom 2s. 6d. per Quarter.

No. 1,751　　　　　FRIDAY, MARCH 13, 1891.　　　　　PRICE ONE PENNY.

# The Tavistock Times

220.　REGISTERED FOR TRANSMISSION AS A NEWSPAPER IN THE UNITED KINGDOM　FRIDAY, FEBRUARY 13, 1925.　THREE-HALFPENCE.

Circulating throughout West Devon and East Cornwall.

# THE TAVISTOCK TIMES
CIRCULATING THROUGHOUT WEST DEVON AND EAST CORNWALL　'Phone: 2042

No. 1,857.　　FRIDAY, MAY 31st, 1957　　TWOPENCE

**Guaranteed Largest Circulation by Far—and Rapidly Increasing**

'Tavistock's fastest growing newspaper'

# The Tavistock Gazette 7p
Established 1857.　And Weekly Advertiser for Devon and Cornwall　Tavistock 5192.
4 January, 1980.　Circulating Tavistock and the Tamar Valley.　No. 6125.

## Tavistock
# CLARION
### An Independent Local Newspaper
Issue No 1　　　　　30 April 1987

# TAVISTOCK TIMES GAZETTE
ESTABLISHED 1857　AN INDEPENDENT FAMILY-OWNED NEWSPAPER　No. 7410
14 Brook Street, Tavistock, PL19 0HD　THURSDAY, MARCH 10, 2005　Telephone: Tavistock (01822) 613666　45p

A selection of mastheads from local newspapers, 1857–2005.

*Right:* In these Pym Street offices, *The Tavistock Gazette* was written and printed from 1907 to 1974. The architect was Arthur Southcombe Parker, who also designed other buildings in the area that was opened up by the construction of Drake Road. After 1974, these offices became Kingdon House, the premises of the Community Association.

*Below: The Tavistock Times* was born in 1920 as a rival to the older *Gazette*. Originally produced in Taylor Square, it moved to Drake Road in 1967. Staff photographer Jim Thorington, a well-loved local character, is seen here outside the newpaper's offices in the 1970s.

In 1983, Dick Lloyd, landlord of the Cornish Arms, revived the office of Town Crier, which had been dormant for sixty-eight years. The council provided a £500 outfit and Lloyd held the office for six years.

Brian Fogg was the editor of *The Tavistock Times* from 1968 to 1973. During this time, the paper, which had become part of the Daily Mirror Group, became involved in the training of young journalists, and young talents such Andrew Morton and Alistair Campbell were nurtured. Here, Fogg is reflecting on the relocation of the printing operation to Ivybridge.

*Above:* In 1977, Kelly College celebrated its centenary. The Bishop of Plymouth, the mayor, the headmaster and Prince Charles stand to attention on the school's front steps as the national anthem is played. Royal stories prove as irresistible to the local press as to the national media. The prince is a well-known local landowner.

*Right:* A June evening in 1985 brought Princess Anne, president of Save the Children, to the town. A tour of the stalls at the charity's fundraising fair was followed by a reception, and the princess left after three hours with a smile and a meat-slicer, the latter bought with the help of a money-carrying detective.

*Left:* Visits from dignitaries have always attracted crowds and press attention. At 2.45 p.m on 3 June 1936, the car carrying King Edward VIII from Princetown paused in Tavistock for five minutes. It was the first occasion that a reigning monarch had visited the town since Charles I in 1644. The small knot around the King comprises Lord Fortescue, the Lord Lieutenant, Messrs Treloar and Wivell, chairman and clerk of the Urban District Council, and Major Holland of the British Legion.

*Below:* General William Booth, the founder of the Salvation Army, was given an enthusiastic reception when he visited the town in 1905. Nine years later his son Bramwell, who had by then taken on his father's role, made a visit, and is shown here addressing a welcoming crowd in Bedford Square.

*Above:* If stories of royalty sell newspapers, so does extreme weather. In March 1891, the area suffered the most intense blizzard on record. This picture of a Princetown-bound train was taken five days after it began its journey and three days after its passengers had been rescued. The staff of *The Tavistock Gazette*, running out of paper, feared that issue No. 1,751 would not be able to be printed, but the discovery in the office of a supply of pink paper made it possible to produce a limited, strange-looking edition (see page 46).

*Below:* Pennington Lane is a narrow road running east-west to connect Plaster Down and Grenofen. The road was blocked when the snows came on 29 December 1962 and was not cleared until a few days before Easter 1963.

*Above:* If members of the royal family are not in sight and the weather is not providing news, then perhaps crime can offer a story. On this quiet stretch of lane between Sowtontown and Cox Tor Farm, on a dark Sunday night in November 1892, a crime of passion, a double murder, was committed. Within days, the area received a great many reporters, sightseers and souvenir collectors.

*Left:* Over the years, Dartmoor prison has provided the local and national media with, on average, one good story each year. Sometimes, though less frequently than of yore, these concerned escaped prisoners. Prison officers normally sought the support of both police and army on such occasions; here, a search is being made of farm buildings on the edge of Tavistock.

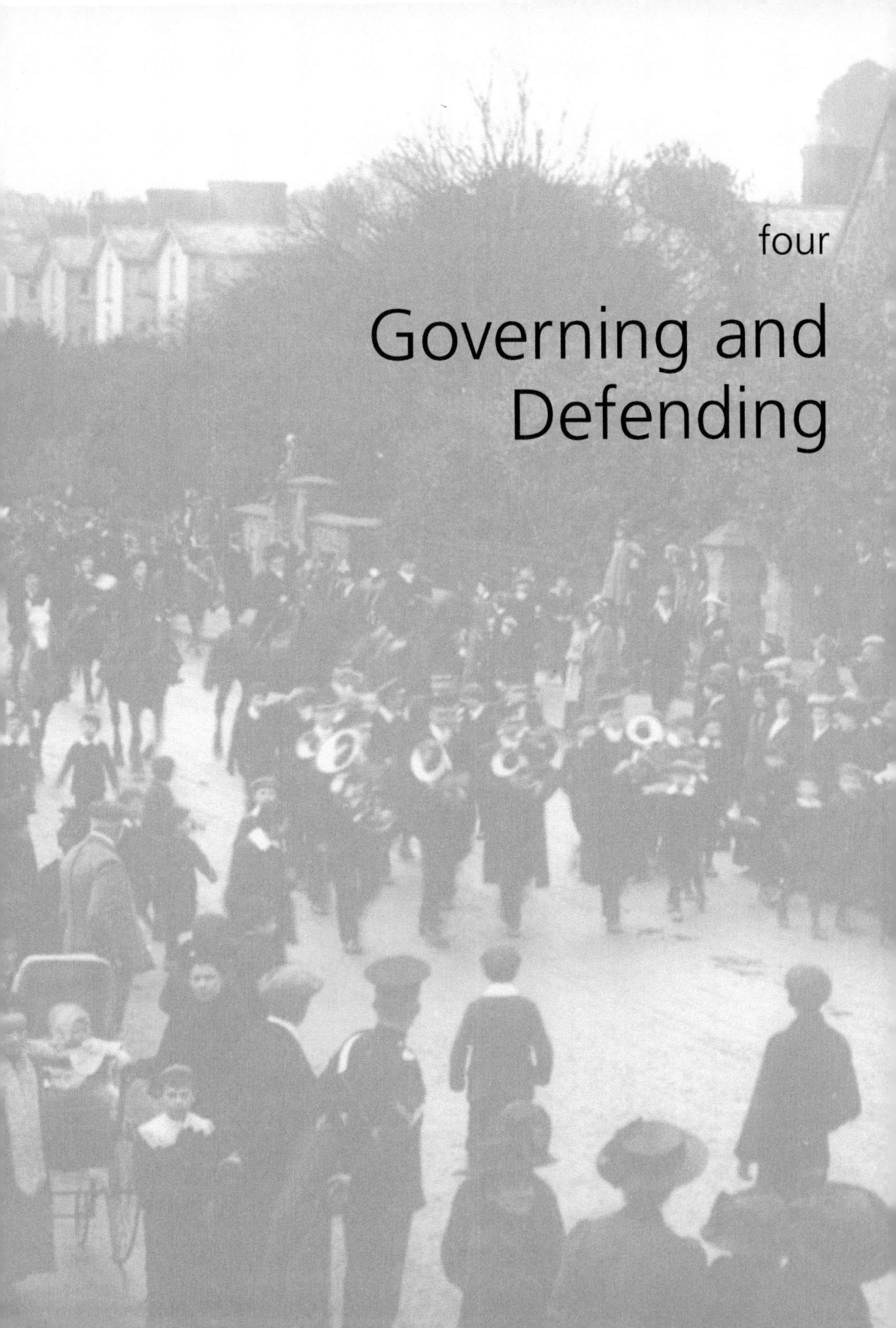

four

# Governing and
# Defending

*Above:* The seventh Duke of Bedford, keeping an eye on his town from atop his Guildhall Square pedestal, is getting one of his periodic facelifts. The Russell family, which holds the title of Duke of Bedford, has never been resident in Tavistock but has influenced the fortunes of the town.

*Left:* The town's coat of arms. The lion is an affirmation of loyalty to the Crown and the fleur-de-lys an acknowledgment of the Virgin Mary as co-dedicatee of Tavistock Abbey. The sheep represents the principal source of the community's original wealth. The shield is occasionally surmounted by a goat which has strayed across from the Russell family arms and, to drive the point home, by a ducal coronet.

*Opposite below:* The town council says thank you to its retiring clerk, Bill Martin, in December 1983. Bill and his wife Joan (seated) are surrounded by council members. From left to right: Bill Smyly, John Philpott, Graham Willis, Roy Reynolds, Norma Woodcock, Margaret Wedd, Betty Bachelor, Robin Fenner, Don Bent (clerk elect), Kevin Wigens (mayor), Albert Piper, Dorothea Pinder, Jenny Haskins, Ted Sherrell, Gordon Foden, Dick Toop.

When Stanley Jenkins was chosen as clerk to the Tavistock Urban District Council in 1947, it was the fourth such appointment in the space of two years. The council needed stability and Jenkins provided it. He retired nearly thirty years later, having presided over a period of major reorganisation and a host of civic events. He is seen here on the right, in October 1958, attending a dinner with Marcel Lambert (left) and Archie Mill (centre), the mayors of Pontivy and Tavistock, to celebrate the formal twinning of the two towns.

In 1968, a vacancy occurred on the Tavistock Council. Party politics was at that period a new and controversial feature of local government at this level. Roy Reynolds decided to contest the seat for Labour. He was opposed by two independent candidates, Robin Start and Edward Gordon. They stand behind the tellers, eagerly watching the count. The result was, from left to right, Reynolds 390, Start 669 and Gordon 155.

*Below:* This postcard, which shows the Tavistock Election Celebration on 25 January 1911, was posted in Tavistock on 30 January 1911. The event being celebrated is the victory, in the previous month, of the Conservative candidate John Spear, who wrested the seat back from the Liberals. Spear's main strength was in the country areas rather than the town, and the size of the crowds in Plymouth Road perhaps reflects that fact.

*Right:* The last person to hold the Tavistock parliamentary seat before its absorption into a larger West Devon constituency was Michael Heseltine, who won two elections here, in 1966 and 1970. He is seen here on the eve of the latter contest, which he won with a majority of 15,449, apparently offering sensible advice to an anxious constituent. At that time, people were taking bets on whether Mr Heseltine would become the third man to both represent Tavistock and make it to No. 10 Downing Street, following two nineteenth-century predecessors, Charles Grey and John Russell. However, it was not to be.

*Below:* The Guildhall, built by the seventh Duke of Bedford in 1848, was used over the years for a variety of public functions but it was designed as a courthouse, with direct access from the police station next door and the cells below. Until 2000, it housed the Magistrates' Court but at the time of writing, its future is in doubt.

In the long line of eminent defenders of the realm, Francis Drake holds a special place because of his role in confronting the Spanish Armada. The statue of the hero, unveiled in his native town in 1883, features on its pedestal three bas-reliefs depicting the game of bowls, the burial and this one, the knighting by Queen Elizabeth. These details were not reproduced on the copy of the statue that adorns Plymouth Hoe.

The French Wars that began in 1793 brought a threat of invasion. One response was the formation of a national movement of Volunteers, based on local units. The Tavistock group was formed in 1799 and was disbanded when the war ended in 1815. It was reformed in 1859 in the face of a renewed threat, real or supposed, from France. This time it had a life of half a century. Its support fluctuated, exceeding 200 for a time before declining in later years. This picture of members of the 22nd (Tavistock) Devon Rifle Corps was taken in the Pannier Market shortly before the Volunteer Movement was replaced by the Territorial Army in 1908.

Members of the 5th Devons, former Territorials, march out of town along Whitchurch Road in August 1914, on the first day of the First World War. Eight of them were not to see their Tavistock homes again. Thomas and Charles Chenhall died in Mesopotamia, Charles Bickle, Thomas Edwards, William Hellier and Charles Spooner in Palestine, and Alfred Pendry and Robert Roberts in France. The town's war memorial bears their names, along with 111 others who fell in the First World War.

A considerable number of men who had been in the local Territorial Force found themselves in India in the early part of the First World War. These men, pictured at their barracks in Barrackpore, Bengal, belonged to the Tavistock Battery before the war and trained at its headquarters at Crelake.

*Above:* The battery at Crelake maintained its identity and strength after the First World War and is shown here in the 1920s. It had the distinction of being the first Territorial Army unit to land in France when the Second World War broke out in 1939. Evacuated at Dunkirk, it reformed and fought in North Africa and then in Italy as part of the 6th Armoured Division.

*Below:* A post-war gathering and celebration, in June 1945, of members of the Nonconformist churches in the town who had been involved in operating the Free Churches Canteen in Russell Street throughout the war. They are standing on the steps of the Wesleyan Methodist chapel in Chapel Street.

The Supreme Commander of the Allied Forces, General Dwight D. Eisenhower, inspects an infantry unit in Bedford Square on 4 February 1944. Tavistock was the headquarters of the US Army's 29th Infantry Division. Prior to D-Day, there were a number of top-level conferences at Abbotsfield and the Manor House, at least one of which was attended by Generals Eisenhower and Montgomery. On the left of the picture is General Omar Bradley and second from the left is Eisenhower's deputy, Air Marshal Sir Arthur Tedder.

Tavistock Grammar School's Head Boy, Dennis Penny, and Head Girl, Brenda Collins, place flowers on the school's memorial, dedicated the day before by the Bishop of Plymouth.

The Whitchurch Home Guard, photographed in 1944. From left to right, back row: Messrs Cook, Hambly, Doidge, Kerswill, Smale, Cooper, McCall, Allen, Munday, Pring, Eva, Collom, Murphy, Roose, Friendship, Chatter. Third row: Messrs Walkington, Toye, Brown, Westcott, King, Vickery, Worden, Titcombe, Maddock, Doidge, Mackenzie, Daw, Vincent, Spurr, Coyte. Second row: Messrs Weeks, Penny, Mudge, Quirk, Hayman, Leach, Gain, Dawson, Marrison, Drake, Sweet, Gaye, Pengelly, Rogers, Angel, Jeffery, Dyer. Front row: Messrs Friend, Kite, Eggington, Cruze, Titcombe, Hodge, Hearn, Willcock, Maddock, Copp, Eddington, Mitchell, Hillman.

Air Training Corps 2312 Squadron at Tavistock School, early 1970s. Squadron Commander Fl. Lt Roy Skipworth looks on as Capt. Bernard Wills presents Cadet Christopher Pratt with the squadron's Sword of Honour. Peter Carthew, left, has received a certificate for outstanding service.

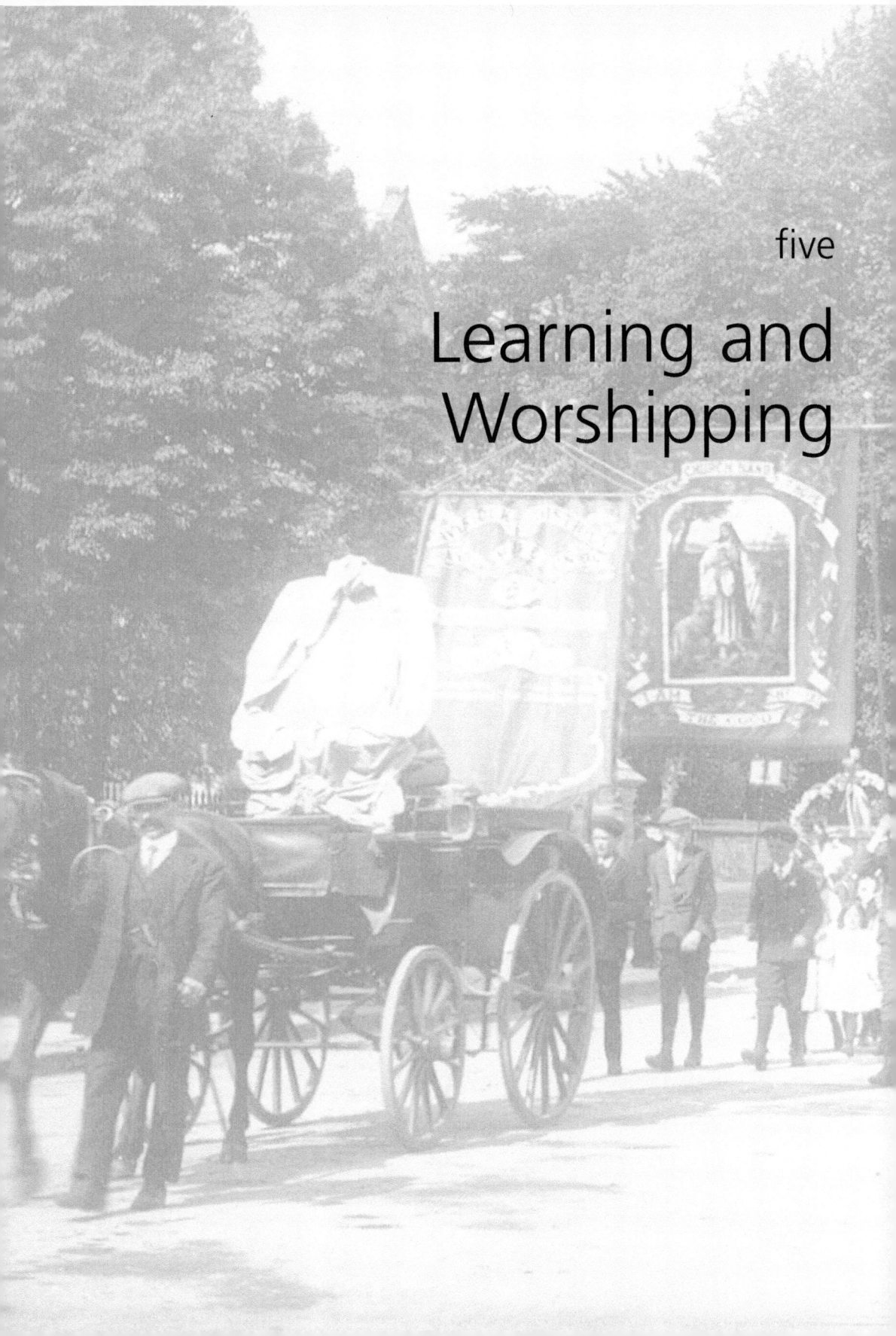

# five

# Learning and Worshipping

The Victorian grammar school in Russell Street, pictured in September 1843, five years into the life of the building. The decorative 'B's and coronets on the building proclaim the identity of the benefactor. One of the figures in the picture could be W.H. Smith, who was a pupil at that time. William Robjohns, the publisher of this picture, had a print-selling business in West Street. The building remained the town's grammar school until 1889.

When, in 1959, the two secondary schools united to form Tavistock School, new premises were provided at Crowndale. The campus of the new school, between the canal and Crowndale Road, is shown in this 1960 postcard. The new buildings take centre stage but the old grammar school premises continue to be used, as do the temporary accommodation and the well-loved pavilion.

The grammar school's Cadet Corps, June 1939. There were only about ninety boys in the school at this time. Behind the drums sit Commanding Officer C.H. 'Spot' Hartley and his assistant W.C. 'Wilf' Rawling, respectively teachers of French and Maths. Most of the lads featured here would be donning other uniforms during the course of the next six years.

In 1952, the grammar school celebrated its quatercentenary and a thanksgiving service was held in the parish church on 25 July, attended by the Bishop of Exeter. Mr Rawling, who had taken over command of the school corps in 1942, led his men to church in style. They are passing one of the school's former homes.

At the grammar school in the 1940s and '50s, the boys played soccer, rugby and hockey in the winter months. The hockey team had the advantage of being coached by Geography teacher D.S. Charleston, a former Indian international player. He is shown here with the 1949 team. From left to right, back row: Mike Parriss, Ken Newnham, Paul Routledge, Fred Sherrell, Gerald Olver, John Rich. Front row: Bob Pate, Bob Pascoe, Dennis Penny, -?-, Richard Wheatley.

K.D. Anderson, headmaster of the grammar school from 1947 to 1953, with his prefects in 1950. From left to right, standing: Graham Willis, Jean Rawling, Bob Pascoe, Sheila Kitley, John Eggins, Roselie Palmer. Seated: Gerald Olver, Dennis Penny, Celia Moore, Ann Myers.

In 1932, when the grammar school moved to Crowndale, girls were admitted for the first time. In the first year, they made up a quarter of the school population, a figure that had grown to half by 1940. Here, in the first summer, is Miss Lowe with her tennis team. From left to right: Margaret Williams, Edna Fellowes, Barbara Nosworthy, Irene Tomkin, Cynthia Knapp, Mary Gilbert.

Only five years on, but projecting a rather bolder image, are members of the 1937 hockey team, with the indomitable and long-serving Miss Nicol. From left to right, standing: Dorothy Pate, Mary Hoyle, Margaret Williams, Martha Mudge, Freda Baker, Dorothy Mills. Seated: Mary Holmes, Christine Medland, Gwen Harding, Iris Ives, Joyce Westcott.

The Revd George Hodgshon, chairman of governors, opens the proceedings at the 1963 speech day at Tavistock School. On his right-hand side is Peter Cook, then in the early stages of an eighteen-year headship. Also in the front row are Norah Taylor, Head of Lower School; Christine Chapman, Senior Mistress; Donald Sleep, Deputy Head; and governors and civic heads.

The four housemasters of Tavistock School, Robert Edwards, 'Hoppy' Hopkins, Geoff Willetts and Percy Perks. These four figures will be immediately recognisable to generations of pupils. The occasion is Hoppy's retirement in the early 1980s, hence the golf clubs.

Late Victorian Tavistock saw a remarkable rise in active support for the cause of temperance. Bands of Hope multiplied, affiliated to the various churches, appealing particularly to the young. A federation of these groups, called the Tavistock and District Band of Hope Union, organised, between 1901 and 1914, a series of annual midsummer demonstrations. This is the last of the series in June 1914, proceeding along Plymouth Road. The sun invariably shone on the chosen days and Tavistock people coined the phrase 'Band of Hope weather'.

May Revels were for some years a regular feature of the local calendar. The first such occasion was in 1921, when this picture was taken. Children at the Dolvin Road School gave displays of singing and dancing in the streets and, as here, in the vicarage garden. Teacher Miss Davis is in charge.

The Dolvin Road School opened in 1847. This picture, dated 1872, shows the boys' school that co-existed, albeit in separate parts of the building, with the girls' and infants' schools. Long-serving headmaster John Loam stands at the back, along with a young curate, for this was a church school. The reasons for the presence of the two ladies and the uniformed officer are unclear.

Tavyside School, founded in 1926 by Mabel Balkwell, had a somewhat nomadic life. It started on Mount Tavy Road and occupied The Priory on Whitchurch Road from 1958 to 1970. Its mistresses and young ladies and gentlemen are pictured here in 1960, when it was owned by Marjorie Kelby and Elsie Elsby. In 1970, it moved to Russell Street and was taken over by Drake's Mead School in 1980.

Young ladies were admitted to Kelly College for the first time in 1975.

*Opposite below:* More than a century on and Dolvin Road houses St Rumon's Infants' School. This is the Red Class in 1990, with headteacher Mrs Mags Long (left) and class teacher Mrs Shirley Davey (right). From left to right, back row: Kate Turner, Thomas Bradbury, Alice Benny. Middle row: Ashley Morton, Edward Steadman, Shane Courtier, Bianca Woodhouse, Oliver Bent, Ian Collacott. Front row: Gemma Wright, Tom Harwell, Claire Davies, Ben Rogers, Elizabeth Score, Tom Medland, Hannah Johnson, Luke Dooley.

Rugby football was the central feature of physical activity in Edwardian public schools. Kelly College's First XV in 1909 included captain A.E. Clarke and, standing to his left, E.D. Skinner, the son of the vicar of Gulworthy, who was to be killed in the First World War. The other members of the team are J.N. Bendyshe, L.I. Burch, G.T. Cindra, B.C.T. Freeland, J.B. Mudge, J.B.S. Notley, A.H. Penny, F.J.M. Shaw, F.C.A.E. Tregoning, C.D. Villares, M.S. Wakefield, V.N.B. Were and J.B. Young.

A quarter of a century on and the 1942 team face the camera. From left to right, standing: D.M. Forbes, R.G. Haines, P.E.H. Ford, J.G. Woodward, P.H. Green, D.H.E. Kirke, P.F. Rendell, J.M. Riddle, M.C. Reed, P.H.B. Hunt, D.A. Jordan, D.T.H. Kent. Seated: R le N Noble, R.H.B. Edwards, D.W.B. Clements. Robert Edwards, who captained the side, was to enjoy a successful teaching career at his old school and later at Tavistock School (see page 68).

The parish church of St Eustachius in 1880. A mid-nineteenth century overhaul had altered the interior by removing the eighteenth-century galleries and pews. Floor-based standards provide gas lighting.

The parish church from the west, 1910.

*Above left:* Many anecdotes survive about Hugh Bickersteth, the saintly, selfless, bicycling bachelor who was vicar from 1918 to 1946. One concerns his offer to give a half-crown to any boy he baptised who had been given among his names that of the church's patron, Eustace. This explains both the chronic poverty of the good pastor and the large number of now elderly Tavistock men called Eustace.

*Above right:* Vicar Bickersteth chats with the Bishop of Exeter, Lord William Cecil, in 1933. They are standing outside the gate of the church hall in West Street, at the opening of which they have just officiated. Bickersteth came from a family of bishops and was himself offered mitres that he declined.

*Opposite above:* Church dignitaries ranging from Benedictine monks to Methodist ministers attend a special service in 1974 to mark the passing of a millennium since the foundation of Tavistock Abbey. They are seen being led into the parish church by the vicar, the Revd Richard Gilpin.

*Opposite below:* Boy choristers in full voice in 1972. From left to right, back row: Nick Perry, David Trick, Robin Derges, Andrew Rogers, Andrew Deas, Philip Newcombe, Paul Gardiner. Front row: David Newcombe, -?-, Paul Willis, Stephen Carter, George Richards, -?-, Andrew Mallard, Nick Ditcher.

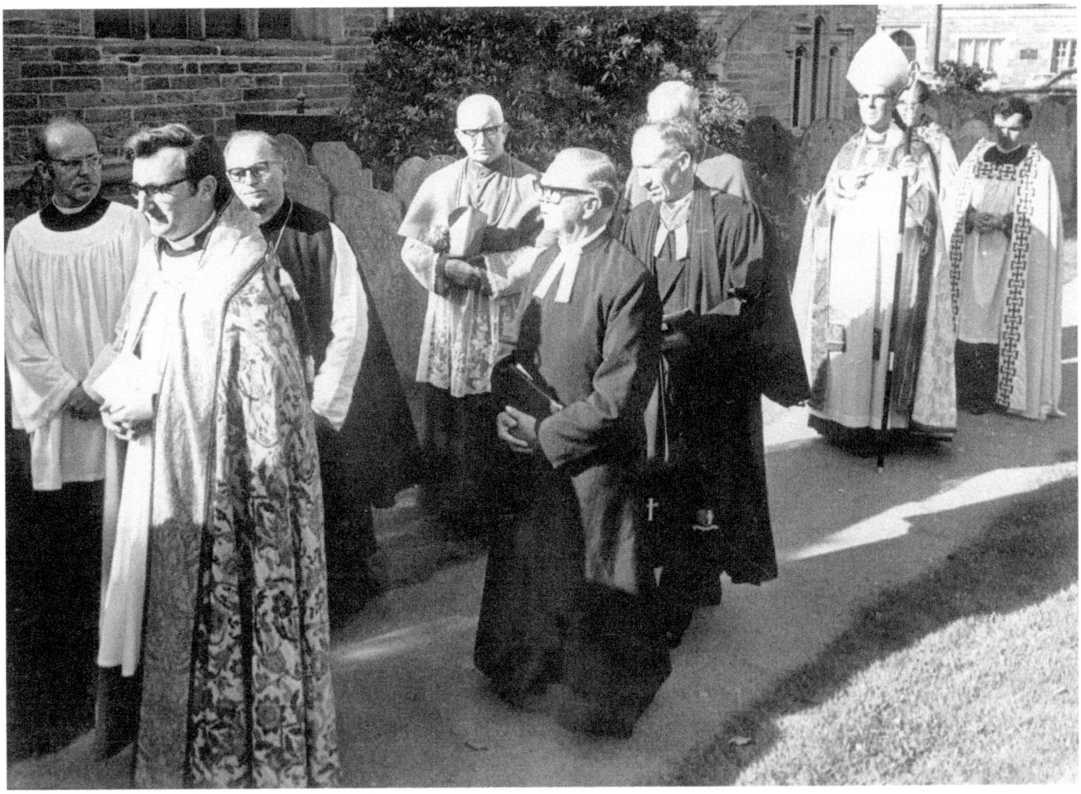

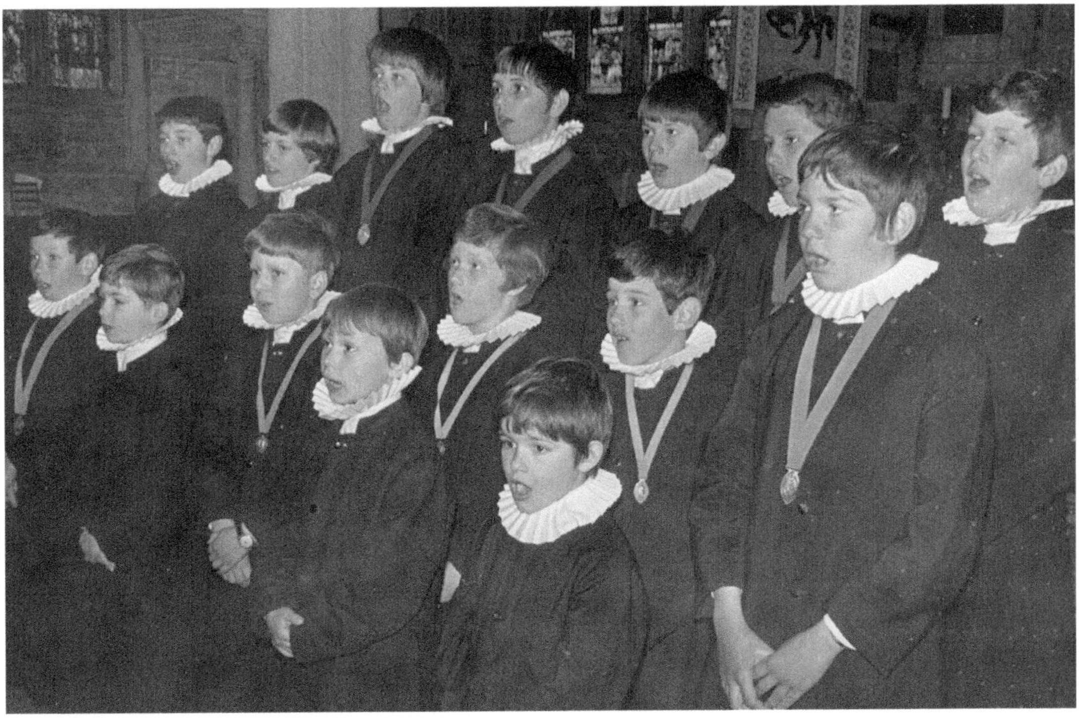

## St. Andrew's, Whitchurch,
### GUILD OF RINGERS.
### RULES.

1. That this Society shall be known as the Whitchurch Guild of Ringers, and shall consist of not more than twelve members.

2. That the members shall meet one night in the week for practice, viz.: on Wednesday, but during Lent on Tuesday evening, and shall ring twice on Sundays (Morning and Evening) at 10-30 a.m. and 6 p.m., and for practice from 7-30 p.m. till 9 p.m. That on Sundays during Lent the Bells shall be only chimed.

3. That there shall be a Captain and Vice-Captain of the Belfry to be elected by the members of the Guild. Such office to be held for six calendar months, viz.: from the first Wednesday in January to the first Wednesday in July, after which they shall retire, but are eligible for re-election.

4. That any young men wishing to become Probationers, must give in their names to the Captain or Vice-Captain, and be approved by them. Such number not to exceed six.

5. That no smoking, swearing, or drinking take place in the Belfry, and that no stranger be admitted into the Belfry during the ringing of the Bells without the consent of the Captain or Vice-Captain.

6. That the Bells shall not be rung should any Parishioner be known to be lying dead or dangerously ill within the vicinity of the Church.

7. That any presents of any kind shall be handed to the Captain for distribution.

8. That these rules shall be strictly enforced, and that any infringement of them shall be dealt with by a Committee consisting of five members, viz.: the Vicar, Captain, Vice-Captain, and two of the members of the guild.

Signed S. W. FEATHERSTONE, M.A.,
January 20th, 1897.                     VICAR OF WHITCHURCH.

That while Harmony is made by the Bells,
Ringers practise Harmony amongst themselves.
Let brotherly love continue,
Do all to the Glory of God.

*Left:* The Guild of Ringers at St Andrew's church, Whitchurch were bound by a set of rules.

*Below:* The Whitchurch ringers in 1924. From left to right, back row: Messrs Headley, Lovell, Skinner, S. Sleeman, Cornish, Dawe, Toye. Middle row: Messrs Roberts, Penhall, Symons, Collins (captain), E. Sleeman, Friend. Front row: Messrs Bickle, Mudge, Brewer.

*Above:* George Thomas, Speaker of the House of Commons and Methodist local preacher, addresses a public audience at an evangelical meeting in the town.

*Below:* St Rumon's in Watts Road was built in 1894. In 1922, it became the home of seven Carmelite nuns who, at the urging of Bishop Kelly of Plymouth, established it as a 'powerhouse of prayer'. The Carmelite house of nuns in full retreat and solitude had a life of seventy-three years but in 1995, with only five resident ageing nuns, the house was closed. It was subsequently demolished and the grounds were redeveloped for residential purposes.

*Left:* The Bible Christian chapel in Bannawell Street was one of three thriving Methodist chapels in the town in the Victorian period. Between 1847 and 1910, it served a congregation who favoured a fundamentalist evangelical form of worship. Between 1910 and 1960, it provided a place of worship for the Plymouth Brethren. It is now used as a builder's store.

*Below:* The Salvation Army made its first appearance in the town in 1882. Renowned equally for its social work, its devotional activities and its music, its band is pictured here in 1923. From left to right, back row: Fred Crocker, Bert Lewis, Fred Tucker, Fred Gregory, Len Tucker, Bill Tucker, Howard Hoar, Harry Tucker, Billy Young. Front row: Joe Gale, Captain Cross, Harry Hoar, Lieutenant Watkins, Bill Lewin, Billy Friend, Bill Stephens.

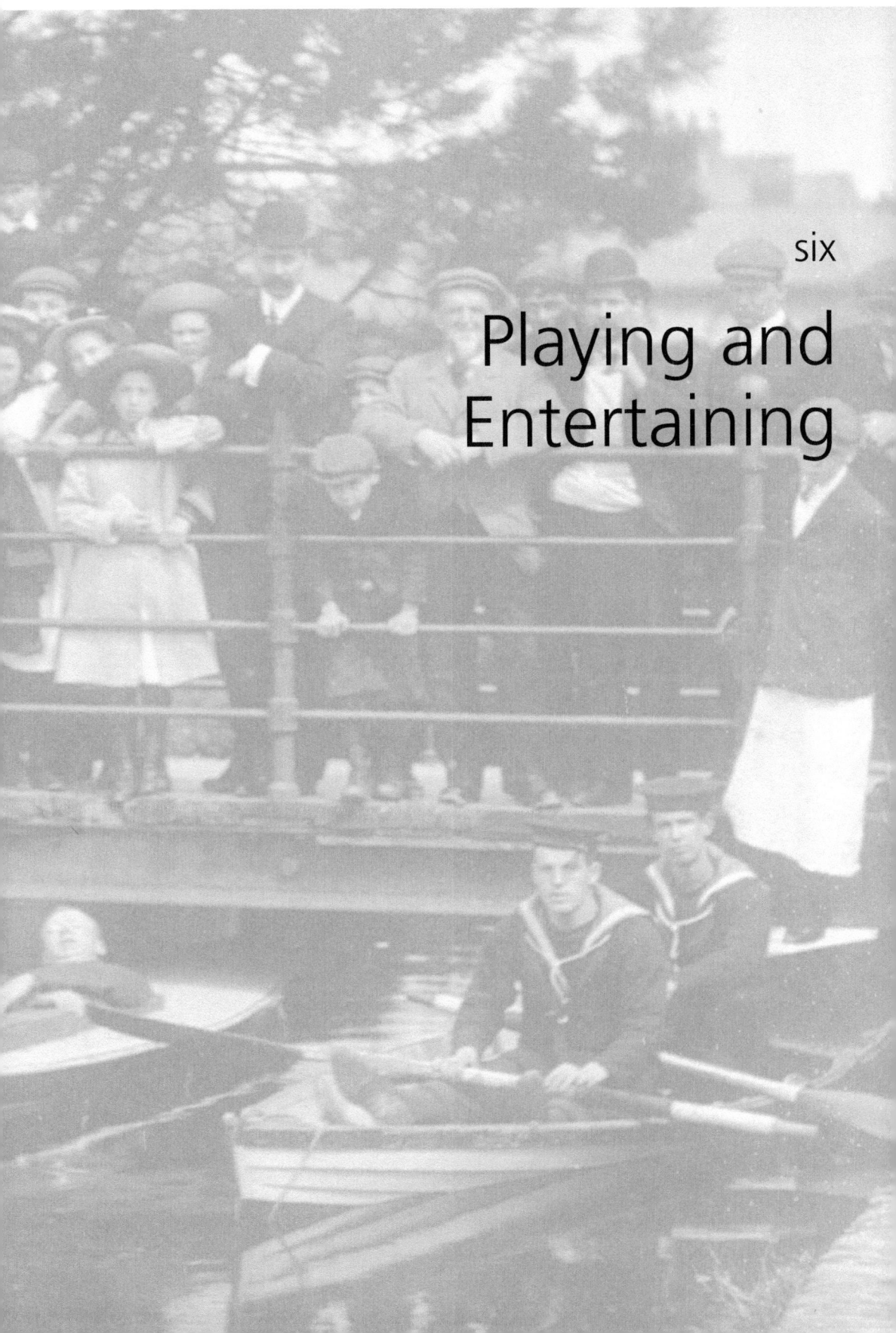

six

# Playing and
# Entertaining

Theatre (*Market Chamber*) *Tavistock*.

## By Particular Desire,

ON THURSDAY 4th. OCTOBER 1827.

WILL BE PERFORMED THE ADMIRED PLAY OF

# The Stranger

| | |
|---|---|
| The Stranger, | Mr. HILLINGTON, |
| Baron Steinfort, | Mr. ADDIS, |
| Francis, | Mr. THOMPSON, |
| Count Winterson, | Mr. CALVERT |
| Solomon | Mr. GAY, |
| Peter, | Mr. STRICKLAND, |
| Tobias, | Mr. JULIAN, |
| Mrs. Haller, | Miss SOMERTON, |
| Countess, | Mrs. GAY, |
| Charlotte, | Mrs. ROGERS, |

"The King and Countryman," Mr. WILLIAMS.

The Soldiers Grave, Mr. ADDIS,

"I never says nothing to Nobody," Mr. THOMPSON.

To Conclude with (for the First Time, at this Theatre,) the FARCE of

# The Rival Valets.

Frank, Mr. STRICKLAND.—Antony Mr. WILLIAMS.—Captain Welford, Mr. HILLINGTON.
Mr. Perkins, Mr. GAY.—Lawyer, Mr. CALVERT.—Clerk, Mr. THOMPSON.
Sophie, Mrs. GAY.—Dorothy Mrs. ROGERS.

The popular Comedy of PAUL PRY, and other Novelties, are in preparation, and will be speedily Produced.

TICKETS may be had, and places for the Boxes taken at Miss HELMS's, and at Mrs. Chave's, Higher Back Street.
Doors open at half past SIX, and Play commences precisely at SEVEN. Second Account at Half past EIGHT.
BOXES 2s. 6d. Half price 1s. 6d.—PIT 1s. 6d. Half price 1s. GALLERY 1s.

A good Fire constantly kept in the Theatre.

From M. CHAVE's, Original Printing Office, Tavistock.

*Left:* The lower of Tavistock's two Market Houses stood in the Bank Square area. It was occasionally used, without the need for major adaptation, by a group of Plymouth players. Chave's, the local printer, produced the handbills and printed and sold the tickets.

*Below:* During the First World War, Mount Tavy House was pressed into service as a neurological hospital providing therapy for hundreds of shell-shocked troops. Some of the patients formed a concert party, specialising in the pierrot shows that were then popular public entertainment, and gave performances in the Town Hall and other venues.

The Tavistock Musical Theatre Company presents regular productions at The Wharf. Originally called the Operatic Society, it has long specialised in operetta and musical shows, presented for many years in the Town Hall. Here, in their 1968 production of *Oklahoma*, Victor Doidge has no difficulty in persuading Joan Macdonald that 'there's a bright golden haze on the meadow'.

The company's 1969 production was *Goodnight Vienna*. Dennis Jackman is receiving the attentions of Dawn Whittaker and Kay Jeffery.

The 1970s saw the formation of a Youth Theatre Group in the Whitchurch Parish Room. A range of young theatrical and musical talent came together to mount a series of performances of high quality. In 1982, it was *Oliver*. From left to right: Ben Portman, Christopher Bowles, Andrew Williams, Edward Rippon, Katherine Duncan, Clare Turner, Marianne Kilpatrick, Sally Anniss.

In 1984, the Youth Theatre Group tackled *Jesus Christ Superstar*. Christ was played by Andrew Williams, who was to find himself, twenty years later, back in Whitchurch as curate at St Andrew's.

*Above:* Morris dancing in the Town Hall in the 1960s.

*Below:* Members of the Rifle Club with some of their trophies. The club was formed in 1905 and met in the Pannier Market until 1935. After that, it used the range in the Drill Hall on Rocky Hill. It moved into its own purpose-built range on 25 November 1970 and the camera was there to record the scene.

Cricket at The Ring, 1953. An all-star side is playing a late-season festival match. Somerset batsman Harold Gimblett, standing sixth from left, scored 81. The host side are seated in the front. From left to right: Walter Spry, Brian Hill, Alec Pethick, Maurice Avery, Bill Colling, Gerry Parsons, Dennis Paull, Eric Davey, Jack Rogers, Bob Featherstonhaugh, Doug Treloar. The club's treasurer, Bernard Kerswill, stands third from left, and its president, Bertie Goss, prepares to umpire.

Members of the Wayfarers Cricket Club gather round their president and benefactor, Mrs Beaver, in 1957. From left to right, standing: -?-, Bob McCall, Rex Murrain, Bill Crocker, -?-, Mike Gill, Brian Perry, -?-, Dennis Crocker, Francis Sprage. Seated: Bill Parkin, Ted Gent, Les Tucker, Tony Glanville, Dennis Towl, Derek Glanville.

An early-season scene at The Ring before a rain-affected game against Buckfastleigh on 4 May 1929. From left to right, standing: Mr Glubb (supporter), Ernie Terrell, Eric Davey, Bill Tucker, Rex Parry, Bray Treloar, Mr Maunder (umpire), Mr Clemo (scorer). Seated: Alfred Treloar, Gordon Parry (captain), Dr Watt (president), Tom Niven, Frank Millman. Frank Bond and Kenneth Terrell are sitting on the ground.

The First XI in 1971, the year in which they won the County Cup. From left to right: Douglas Treloar, Maurice Craze, Phil Treseder, David Ewings, Eric Jarman, Geoff Husband, Tony Clapp, Tim Redman, Hilton Jones, Evan Kemp, Derek Pethick.

*Left:* Jack Davey is the most illustrious sportsman that Tavistock has ever produced. His thirteen seasons with Gloucestershire were sandwiched between periods when he played for his home-town club. He belonged to a cricket dynasty, his father and grandfather both having been club stalwarts. On 29 September 1968, he unveiled a clock on the pavilion at The Ring in memory of his father, Eric. Looking on is the club chairman, Jack Taylor.

*Below:* The Ring, home of Tavistock Cricket Club since its formation in 1849, is pictured here in 1900. The postcard was produced and sold by Arthur Holden, who was the club's professional, before starting a stationery business in King Street.

The Tavistock Association Football Club was in its fourteenth season when this picture was taken at its Torlands ground in 1902. The club officials flanking the players are, from left to right, Messrs Harwood, Snow and Bellamy. The players are standing in traditional soccer 5-3-2-1 formation. From left to right, the forwards are Merrifield, Williams, Hawkey, Knott and Craze, the half-backs are Dealve, Holman and Cox, the full-backs are Barkell and Spooner, and the goalkeeper is Cole. Standing back left is the reserve, Bartlett.

Tavistock AFC players and officials, 1927. In that season, the club, then resident at Sandy Park, erected a grandstand to hold 100 supporters. They also reached the final of the County Cup. This picture may have been taken at Plymouth, where, in front of 7,000 spectators at Home Park, the 'lambs' went down to the Royal Naval Barracks in the final.

*Above:* The Tavistock team in the 1996/97 season, at the club's most recent home, Langsford Park. From left to right, standing: P. Lowe (secretary), J. Dawe, D. Babb, N. Minhinnick, D. Symons, A. Brenton, S. Shaw, A. Godfrey, C. Gott, D. Halfyard, L. Mewton (physiotherapist), E. Pinch (committee member). Seated: J. Hajiyianni, R. Campbell, S. Metters (manager), R. Fenner (chairman), J. Collins (assistant manager), M. Wall, T. Bason.

*Below:* After false starts in the 1870s and 1920s, the Tavistock Rugby Club was established in 1969. For the first twenty-one years, until the acquisition of land at Sandy Park, it had no permanent home. This game against Dartmouth in November 1974 took place at Mary Tavy, one of its temporary residences.

*Right:* The tennis club's first home was at Anderton Lane in Whitchurch, close to the railway line. Founded in 1921, the club had originally just one grass court in the grounds of Anderton Cottage. By the time this picture was taken in the 1940s, the adjacent bowling green had become a second court. Hard courts were added in 1956 and 1967.

*Below:* In 1962, Stumbles was put out to grass in The Meadows after a lifetime of service on Devon's roads. It became a well-loved but gradually deteriorating plaything, before being taken into care by the newly formed Robey Trust in 1983.

*Above:* Sydney Pearce produced the picture for this postcard. The date is 11 November 1911, the place Pitland Corner, off Brentor Road, and the occasion the opening meet of the Lamerton Foxhounds, a local pack formed in 1880 and mastered for many years by H.M. Sperling.

*Below:* In 1905, the golf club built a new clubhouse to replace the accommodation that had been built when the club was founded in the previous decade. The 1905 clubhouse, shown here, occupied a site on the opposite side of Down Road from the present clubhouse, built in 1915.

In the early years of the twentieth century, the stretch of canal through The Meadows from the wharf to Fitzford and beyond was used for recreational boating, though the low bridges were significant hazards. The waterway had not carried commercial traffic since 1873.

It would be strange if the town that produced Francis Drake did not have a thriving bowling club. These men are stalwarts of the club in play in 1970. Roland Bailey gives his judgement and Wilf Rawling looks as if he may be ready to agree. The gentleman behind looks as if he will take a little more persuading.

A women's hockey squad in the 1970s. In 1949, the hockey club was revived after a ten-year gap and moved into new premises at Birchwood Terrace. It offered facilities for both men's and women's teams.

A triumph for Tavistock's lady golfers, as they show off a trophy outside the clubhouse in the mid-1970s. From left to right: Sue Gowing, Connie Burridge, Marjorie Greening, Grace Tucker, Sharon Williams, Pat Turnball, Barbara Berryman.

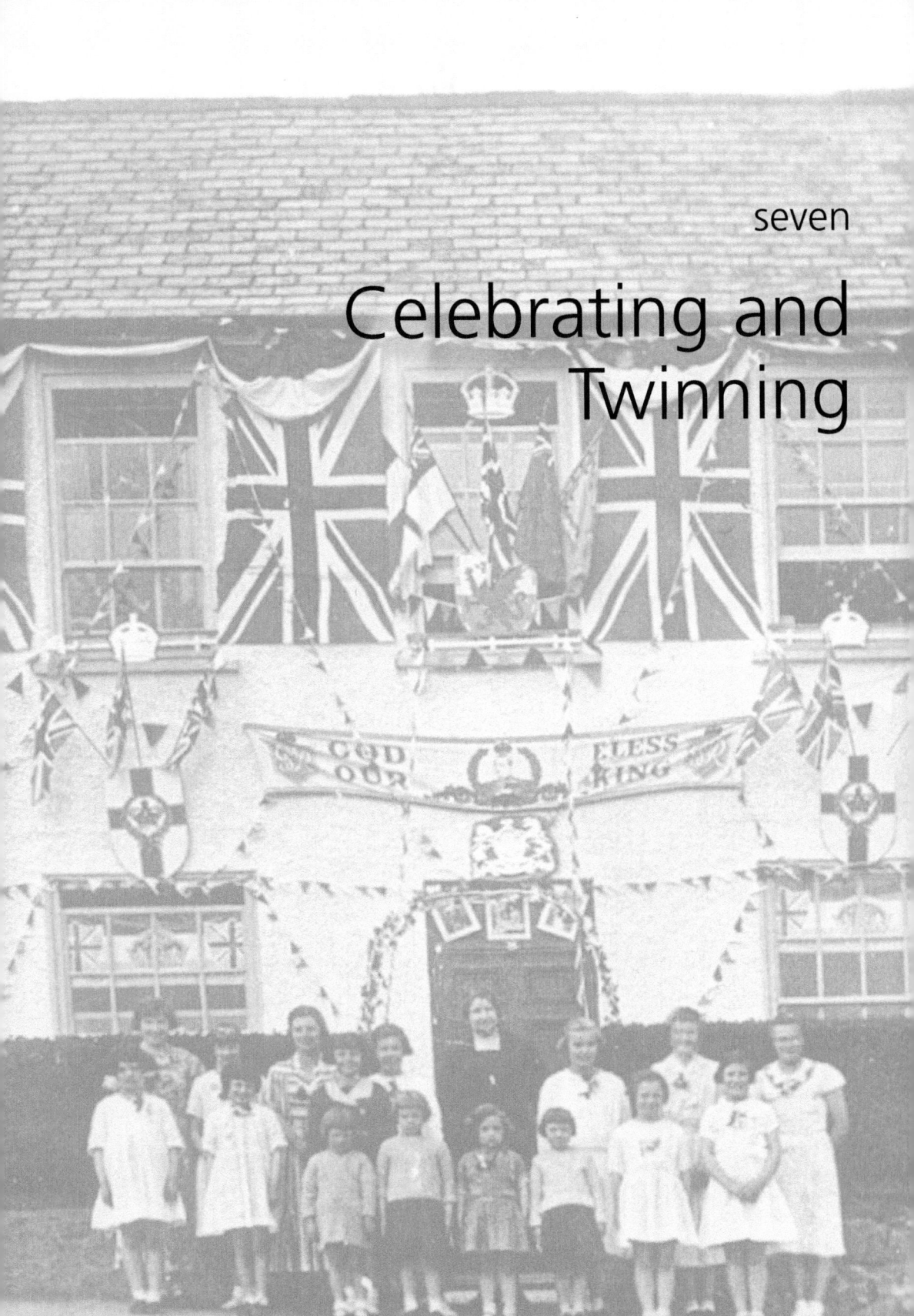

# seven

# Celebrating and Twinning

*Above:* Tavistock's French twin town is Pontivy, in the heart of Brittany. A ceremony takes place regularly at the biennial fair in Pontivy, when the mayors of the town's British and German twins are invited to participate in the laying of wreaths at the war memorial. On this occasion, Mayor Masson is flanked by Mrs Woodcock of Tavistock and Herr Muller of Wesseling.

*Left:* During the Second World War, Pontivy was occupied from 18 June 1940 to 4 August 1944. On the day of liberation, the first tricolour to be hoisted in the town was the one pictured here. When, in 1958, Pontivy and Tavistock twinned, the flag was given to Tavistock as a symbol of common endeavour and friendship. It has an honoured place in the Council Chamber.

*Above:* In 1976, a civic delegation from Tavistock visited the German town of Celle to make arrangements to build on the many contacts between the two towns that had developed over the previous twenty-four years. Mayor Norna Beadle, Town Clerk Bill Martin and Councillor Ted Jago are greeted in Celle Town Hall by the mayor, Dr Horstman. Sadly, Mr Jago died during the visit.

*Right:* The formal twinning ceremony between Tavistock and Celle took place in Bedford Square in 1977. The two mayors, Messrs Philpott and Horstman, hold the copy of the twinning charter that is now exhibited in the Mayor's Parlour.

Both the royal Silver Jubilees of the twentieth century were celebrated in style. In February 1935, a suitably decorated Town Hall hosted a ball to mark George V's Jubilee.

Queen Elizabeth's Silver Jubilee in 1977 was the occasion for a full programme of events, particularly involving children. Mayor John Philpott toured the events. His wife, Peggy, received a bouquet at this party.

The four coronations that occurred between 1902 and 1953 saw similar programmes of activities, with a children's tea party being one of the centrepieces. This party in the Pannier Market was held to celebrate the Coronation of George VI in 1937.

The girls in the Scattered Home at the foot of Spring Hill celebrate the 1937 Coronation with their foster mother. The house accommodated fourteen girls, whose ages ranged from three to fifteen. When they left school and went into service, they were given outfits costing up to £5 but their wages were kept for them in the post office until they were sixteen. In 1940, the girls were dispersed to other homes and the house became a Scattered Home for boys.

Flags, flowers, best frocks and posh tuxedos. It can only mean the Hunt Ball. The ladies' fashions reveal immediately that we are in the Town Hall in 1928.

Some Merrivale families prepare for a day of sunshine and fun in 1921. The annual charabanc trip to the seaside was part of most people's experience in Tavistock in the early part of the twentieth century. It seems that there was not a church, Sunday school, business, club, school, organisation or street that did not organise such an outing.

For much of the twentieth century, the message 'Lennard's World-Famed Boots and Shoes' adorned the façade of No. 2 West Street. The business put down its Tavistock roots just before the First World War. Members of the staff are shown in a tableau presentation at one of the carnivals of the 1920s.

Fifty years on its carnival time again, and the atmosphere is unchanged. The 1970s saw a thriving local film society, advertising itself here with the support of some of our great cinema characters.

At the 1921 carnival, the winner of the cup in the section promoting the town's trades was the carriage fitted out as a blacksmith's shop. The blacksmith, F.W. Redstone, is standing by his apprentice, James Acton, who holds the cup. They borrowed the cart from Charles Green, the coal merchant. The three of them are celebrating their victory in Market Road after the procession.

Ever since the first carnival in 1885, the prime purpose has been to raise money for local charities. In the inter-war years, the chief beneficiary was the cottage hospital. Here the local fire brigade is preparing to do its bit for the cause, and takes the opportunity to show off its motorised, albeit still solid-tyred, transport.

The Goose Fair, which has its origins in the Michaelmas Fairs of the sixteenth century, is the day in October when the world comes to Tavistock. This is the 1912 Goose Fair. Most people enjoyed themselves but not Mr George Moon, who complained in the local newspaper that 'the worst cases of bastardy are attributed to this annual debauchery'.

The streets in the town centre are transformed for the Goose Fair and cars are banned. Geese are hard to find these days but the Golden Gallopers on the carousel are popular with young and old.

BOROUGH OF      TAVISTOCK.

## Prince of Wales' Marriage Celebration

It being resolved that TUESDAY next, the 10th of MARCH, be observed as a

# GENERAL HOLIDAY

The Committee beg to announce the following Programme:

THE DAY WILL BE USHERED IN WITH

## BANDS OF MUSIC, RINGING OF BELLS, &C

At half-past Ten, a.m.,

# A PROCESSION

Will form in front of the NEW HALL, and proceed through the Town in the following order, viz

THE MEMBERS OF THE

## 22nd Devon Volunteer Rifle Corps

ACCOMPANIED BY THEIR BAND.

THE PORTREEVE, MACE BEARERS, AND GENTLEMEN
OF THE COMMITTEE.

CARRIAGES WITH DINNER RECIPIENTS.

THE TAVISTOCK TEETOTAL BRASS BAND,

Followed by the

## ODDFELLOWS AND FORESTERS

Who will appear with their Banners and Insignia.

THE TAVISTOCK FIFE AND DRUM BAND.

MEMBERS OF THE PHILANTHROPIC SOCIETY

And such Trades as may be desirous of joining.

At Twelve o'clock,

A Feu de Joie will be given by the Volunteers

In celebration of the auspicious event.

At One o'clock,

## 400 Aged Persons will Dine together

IN THE NEW MARKET.

At half-past Two o'clock,

## THE SCHOOL CHILDREN

Accompanied by their instructors will Form in front of the New Hall, and with the Bands,
Carriages, &c., proceed through the principal streets.

At Four o'clock,

# 2,000 CHILDREN

Will partake of TEA in the New Market.

At half-past Six o'clock,

## The New Hall will be Illuminated.

## A TORCH-LIGHT PROCESSION

Will be arranged, and accompanied by the BANDS, march through the Town; after
which they will proceed to Whitchurch Down, where

## A LARGE BONFIRE

Will be kindled at half-past Eight o'clock, when

Cheers for the Prince and Princess, and God save the Queen

Will terminate the Public Proceedings.

## May Pole Dancing and other Sports

Will be continued at intervals.

All Persons taking part in the above, are requested to appear in Rosettes of Coventry Ribbon.

To give all Parties an opportunity of participating in the above Festivities, the Inhabitants are
kindly invited by the Portreeve to Close their Establishments throughout the day.

By order of the Committee:

G. H. SMITH, Hon. Secretary.

In 1857, *The Tavistock Gazette* expressed a widespread view when it argued that the town needed 'a spacious and decent room for the social gatherings of the people'. Francis, the seventh Duke of Bedford, was a good listener and planning began, with steward John Benson, Bedford estate surveyor Theophilus Jones and architect Edward Rundle playing leading parts. Construction work began in March 1860. Three years later, on 10 March 1863, with the project still incomplete, it was decided that the New Hall, as it was to be called for some years, could, for the first time, be made the centrepiece of a celebration. The occasion was the marriage of Edward, Prince of Wales and Princess Alexandra of Denmark. A striking innovation was the lighting of the façade by gas. This must have been, on that evening, an impressive sight, captivating both residents and visitors, as it has continued to do ever since. The official opening took place eleven months later, in February 1864. Tavistock at last had its 'spacious and decent room'.

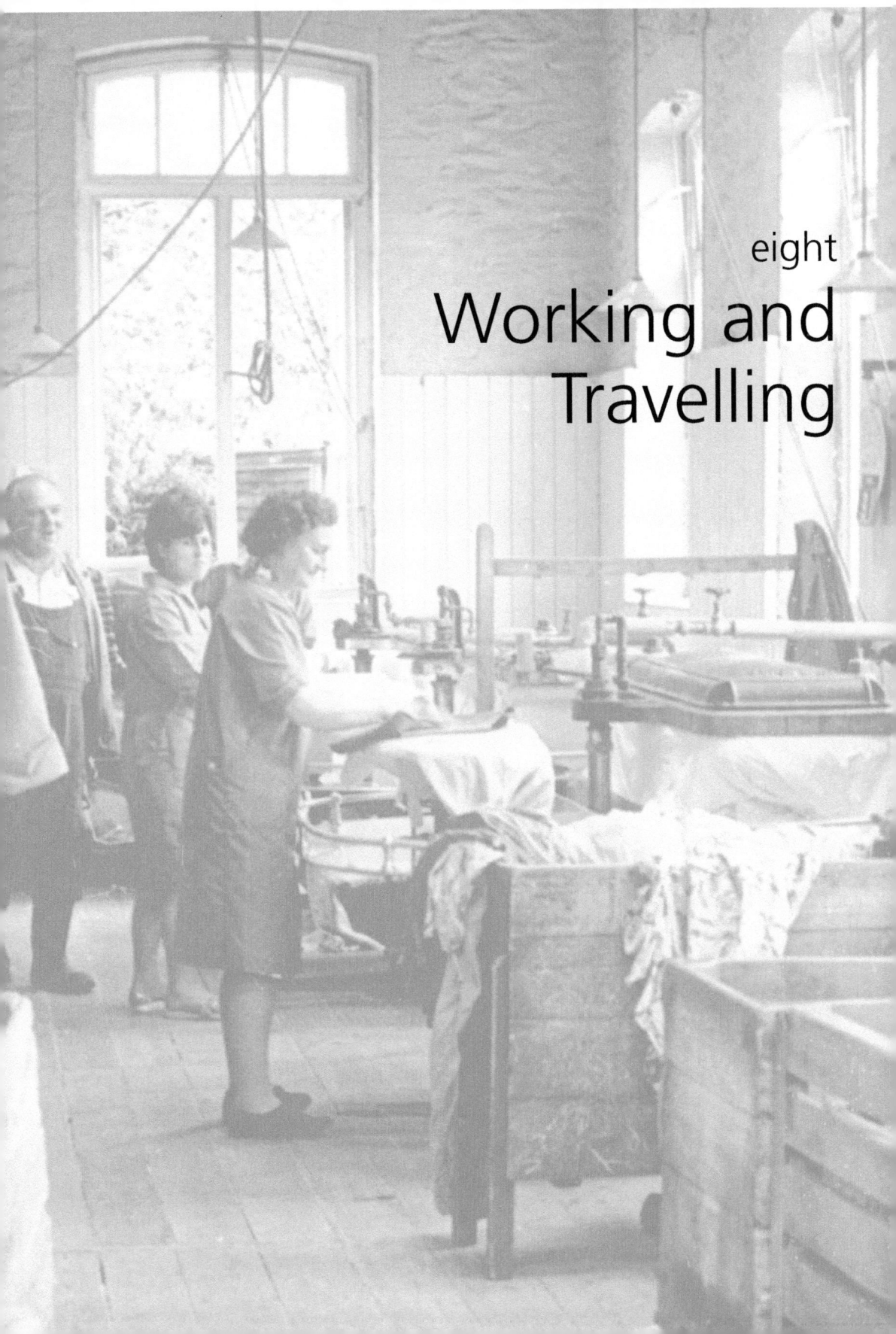

eight

# Working and Travelling

# LOWER PENNATON,

**Parish of Whitchurch,**

About Three Miles from Tavistock, with Stations on the G. W. Ry., and L. & S. W. Ry.

**Sale of 110 Sheep and 25 Bullocks.**

# GLANVILLE & SON

Are instructed by Mr. JOHN DOIDGE, (who is declining Business,) to Sell by Auction, at Lower Pennaton,

ON MONDAY, 8TH OF AUGUST, 1904,

THE UNDERMENTIONED

# LIVE STOCK,

VIZ:

**Sheep :-** 50 Breeding Ewes, 45 Ewe and Wether Lambs, 12 Wethers, 3 Rams.

**Bullocks:-** 6 Cows in Milk and 1 in Calf (2 lately renewed), 2 Heifers 3 years old, 4 Steers 3 years old, 4 Steers 2 years old, 4 Heifer Yearlings, 3 Steer Yearlings, and 2 Calves.

**Luncheon at 12-30, by Ticket, at 1s. each, returnable to Purchasers.**

SALE TO COMMENCE AT 2 P.M.

Dated Auction and Valuation Offices, [illegible], West Street, Tavistock, July, 1904.

CHAVE, PRINTER, &c. TAVISTOCK.

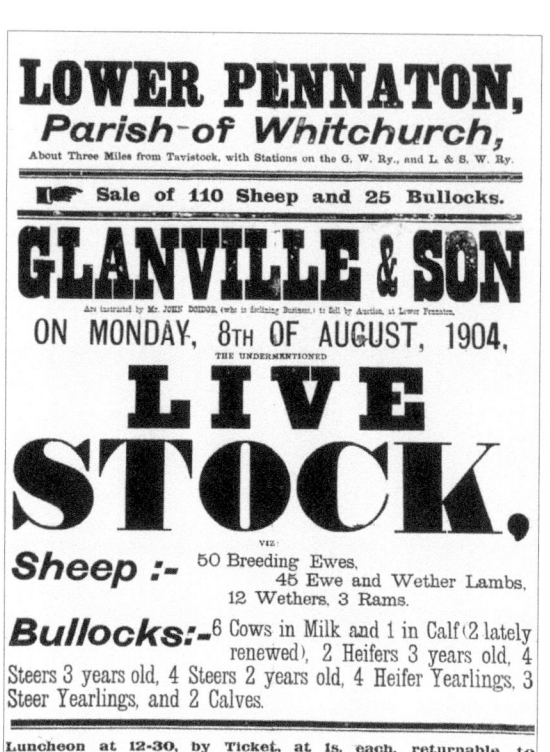

*Left:* Agriculture has always played a significant part in the economy of Tavistock, partly because a good deal of farming is carried on in the parish, partly because of the market and partly because of the dependence of the town's trade on the custom of local farming interests.

*Below:* A familiar sight in the town. It is an appealing sight, except perhaps to those sitting in their cars on Plymouth Road. Destination market?

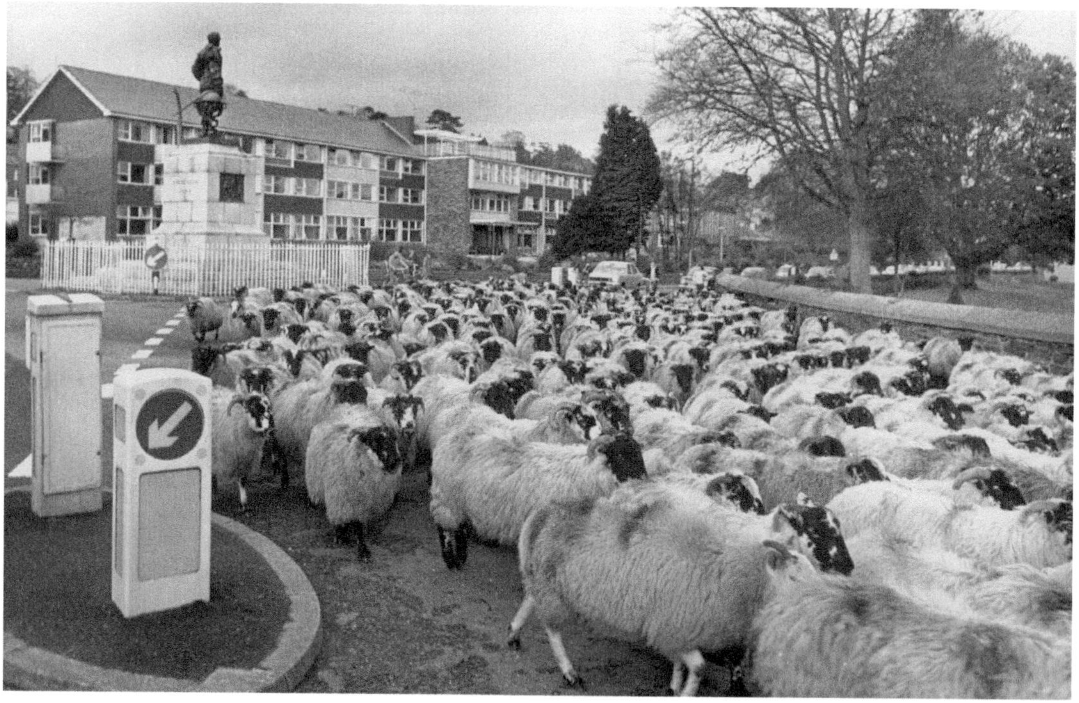

Bill Toye farmed at Whiteacres and this was his wartime tractor. Village boy David Gordon, seen here sitting behind the wheel, recalls that 'as it had to run on the cheap fuel, not petrol, it was warmed up on a small amount of precious petrol before being turned over to the cheap stuff. There were always bangs and groans from the complaining engine before it burst into life with clouds of choking black smoke'.

*Below:* Until the 1980s, the pre-Christmas fatstock show was held in the Pannier Market. Centre stage and taking the plaudits is the 1975 prize bull. Behind him is Mayor Norna Beadle, wearing a hat, and next to her Lady Morley and her husband, the Lord Lieutenant.

This woolcombing factory operated from 1899 to 1965. Wool is Tavistock's oldest industry and was for centuries a central feature of trade and employment. There are many reminders of this fact in the town. For example, the coat of arms contains the banded sheep and the church has an aisle built with the profits of the trade.

In 1899, the Hayle-based firm of Hosken, Trevithick, Polkinghorne and Co. acquired an old foundry building at Parkwood, which had been unused for five years, and fitted it up with woolcombing machinery. The factory is shown here between the wars. Its closure in 1965 drew a final line under a chapter of local history that had lasted for seven centuries.

The opening of the Tavistock and District Laundry in 1899 was widely welcomed, not only because it provided a service but because it offered jobs at a time when the town was suffering a post-mining depression. Built by two brothers called Spooner, the laundry was sold in 1921 to entrepreneur and public figure William Gulley. He, in turn, sold it to Lord Carnock, whose family ran it until its closure in the 1970s. It is seen here in its final days.

Some of the employees of the laundry (the workforce was predominantly female) prepare the firm's publicity float for a carnival between the wars. Ladies who worked in the laundry during that period recall starting at the age of fourteen and working forty-four hours a week for twopence halfpenny an hour.

Mining was a major factor in the local economy for centuries and its impact on the landscape is still evident. This wooden aqueduct was built near Double Waters during the sixteenth century to carry water to the workings of the Virtuous Lady and Lady Bertha mines. This photograph was taken around 1890 and shows how water leaking from the aqueduct has formed icicles.

The great mining enterprises of the nineteenth century included the Devon Great Consols mine, at that time the most productive copper mine in the world. This lunar landscape at Wheal Josiah is part of its physical legacy. Tavistock's key role in mining history is reflected in its designation as a medieval stannary town, or administrative centre of the tin-mining industry.

Gem mine, the remains of which are seen here around 1880, was situated a short distance from where Magpie Bridge crosses the river Walkham. The dominant feature is the Walkham Viaduct, constructed by the great engineer I.K. Brunel to carry the Great Western Railway line over the river between Tavistock and Horrabridge.

Taviton is an ancient hamlet on the eastern edge of the town. The Taviton brook, a tributary of the Tavy, has been a major source of power over the centuries. In the late fifteenth century, for example, there were three tucking mills operating here. This Sydney Pearce postcard captures the scene half a millennium later.

The beginning: Tuesday 21 June 1859 was the day when the railway came to Tavistock. The occasion, with the town en fête, was not caught on camera but T.V. Robins made a sketch of the scene at the railway station. It appeared three weeks later in the pages of the *Illustrated London News*.

The end: The railway line that was inaugurated with such a flourish on a midsummer afternoon in 1859 closed with a snowy whimper in midwinter 1962, when, on 29 December, the last scheduled journey was abandoned in a blizzard. After its closure, the railway bridge that took the line across the foot of Whitchurch Road was demolished.

The loss of the GWR station in 1962 left Tavistock with one rail lifeline, the old London and South Western Railway route between Waterloo and Plymouth. Its station, on Kilworthy Hill, is shown here. The camera is looking westward towards the viaduct and Glanville Road.

Ten years later and it's a very different scene. The last passengers passed through the station on 5 May 1968. The site was later developed to accommodate the offices of West Devon Borough Council. The stationmaster's house, on the left, was renamed Beeching's Folly.

*Left:* The construction of the 4½ mile canal linking the Tavy at Tavistock with the Tamar at Morwellham was begun in August 1803 and completed in June 1817. Engineering problems that had to be overcome included crossing the river Lumburn, providing an inclined plane to connect the end of the waterway with the port of Morwellham and, most challenging of all, tunnelling through Morwell Down. This is the southern entrance to the 1½ mile tunnel, pictured during the annual inspection of the canal.

*Below:* The Tamar port of Morwellham, the Tavistock Canal's destination. On the day of the official opening of the canal, 24 June 1817, 400 invited guests made the trip aboard iron boats. Ships in the dock greeted them with twenty-one-gun salutes, toasts were drunk to the success of the enterprise, and celebrations continued for the rest of the day.

*Right:* This old milestone, one of many that adorn our roadsides, stands on Whitchurch Down, near the top of Green Lane. Inscribed on one side is 'I/T', which means '1 mile to Tavistock'. In one of the dafter interpretations of the Removal of Direction Signs Order of 1940, the milestone was removed and hidden but was later restored.

*Below:* In 1863, *The Tavistock Gazette* printed an angry editorial complaining about the turnpike trusts and their toll-houses: 'We are engirdled by these repulsive institutions'. For more than a century, all the main roads out of the town were subject to toll payments. The toll-houses survive. This one, on Parkwood Road, dates from 1817, when the new road was built to replace the narrow, bumpy Exeter Road.

A bus driver and conductor pause for a smoke before the journey to Plymouth in a quiet Bedford Square in the early 1930s. In 1929, the Western National Company was formed by the amalgamation of two older bus companies. It became the predominant provider of public road transport around Tavistock.

A project promoted by the Western National Company and the county council reached fruition in March 1958, when the bus station on Plymouth Road was formally opened. It is shown here just a few years later.

*Opposite above:* The quality of public transport declined in the last third of the twentieth century because of the huge increase in car ownership. Robert Carr was one businessman who both anticipated and responded to this trend. His earlier premises in Parkwood in the 1920s and Drake Road in the early 1930s were followed by a settled home on Plymouth Road, shown here in its last days.

*Opposite below:* To people like Harry Hobbs, driving was a pleasure and a sport. His 1960s hand-built machine featured two front wheels from a motorcycle, a Ford Two engine and a fan in front of the bonnet.

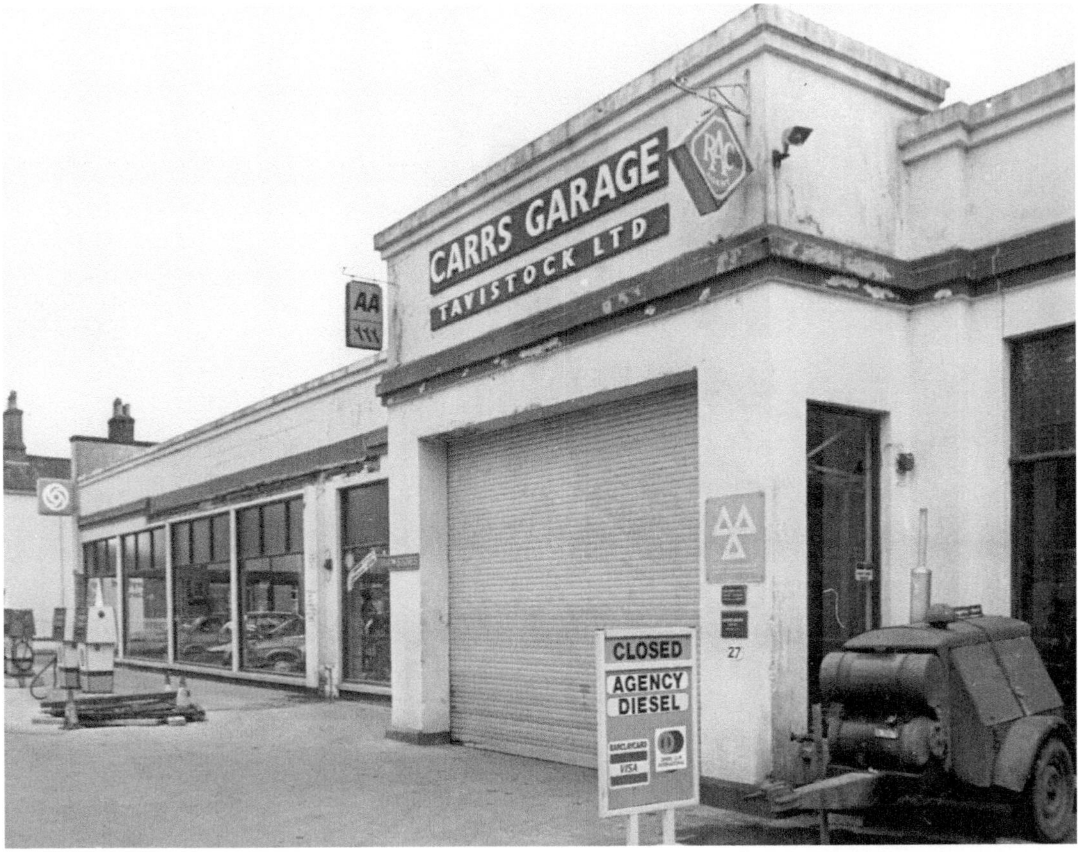
CARRS GARAGE
TAVISTOCK LTD
AA
CLOSED
AGENCY
DIESEL
VISA
27

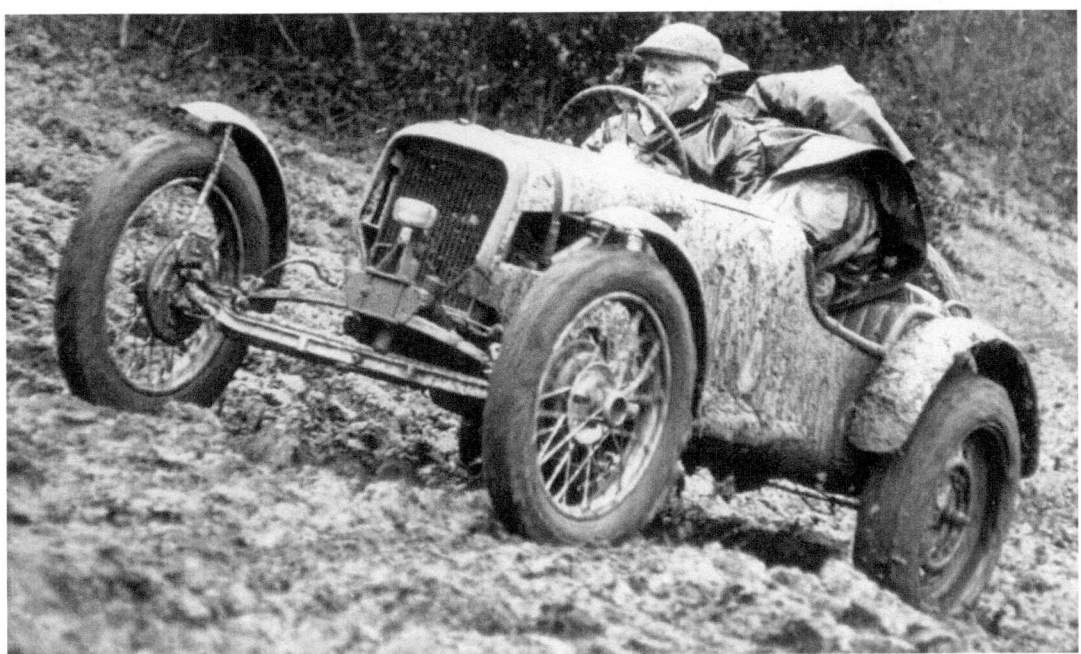

The 1970s was a decade plagued by problems of oil supplies. Ian Green comes to terms with petrol rationing.

The 1970s also saw some outbreaks of industrial unrest. In 1978, workers in local government went on strike. The action involved Tavistock's dustmen, gathering here in Bedford Square.

# nine

# Trading and Competing

Brook Street. At No. 30, on the corner of Brook Street and Vigo Bridge Road, Charles J. Frost, greengrocer and fruiterer, ran a well-known business from the 1930s. In 1938, he married Hilda Gawman, a local girl. As the century came to its close, she was in good health and living within a stone's throw of the shop.

*Below:* Brook Street. Herbert Brown traded here from 1915 to 1930, operating a dairy and restaurant which gave employment to twenty-five people.

West Street. On Goose Fair Day in 1900, Albert Thomas Sweet opened a tailoring business on the north side of the road, at No. 83. Over the years, he expanded both the scope of the business and the premises. After his death in 1952, control passed first to his widow Edith and then to his son Thomas. It remained in the family until its sale in 1972.

West Street. This photograph, taken from the foot of the south side of the street around 1970, shows S. Truman's fruiterers and florists, W. Willis' butchers and Lennard's shoe shop facing the Cornmarket across the road. In the early part of the twentieth century, this street accommodated fifty-two businesses.

This easily recognisable town centre building features pillars that may originally have adorned the ill-fated classical library building in Bedford Square. Charles Beckerleg had his electrical emporium here in the 1960s.

Before the Beckerleg era, his premises housed a family business founded by John German and operating from the 1870s to the 1930s. Makers of boots and shoes, the firm was particularly proud of its Dartmoor boot, which it advertised as 'the strongest boot in the world'.

*Above:* The north side of Duke Street in 1960 features Woolworths, a music shop and Bond's garage. Charles Bond bought premises on Vigo Bridge Road in 1919 and began an association with the Ford company. Under Charles's two sons, Norman and Lewis, the Duke Street showroom was opened, continuing there until 1970.

*Below:* The staff employed by Bond's in the 1960s, pictured in their Duke Street premises. From left to right, back row: C. Matthews, M. Palmer, L. Phare, R. Pengelly, W. Trethewey, D. Evans, K. Luscombe, A. Friendship, G. West. Middle row: J. Freeman, J. Stone, M. Kelland, H. Boney, K. Pearce, S. Dodd, F. Hardesty, G. Williams, S. Hardwell, W. Heppenstall, R. Hicks, T. Cackett. Front row: M. Yelland, J. Burridge, A. Greenstreet, J. Beynon, N. Bond, C. Bond, L. Bond, N. Baker, D. Carter, B. Jessop, F. Bray.

A visit to Creber's store is, for many people, one of the highlights of a day in Tavistock. Since its foundation in 1881, the business has expanded but has remained true to a set of principles related to quality and service which continue to make it a distinctive place to shop. Two generations of the family appear in this 1979 picture, as Robert (left) prepares to take over as managing director from his father, Norman (second left).

Across the road from Creber's, on the north side of Duke Street, Keymarkets opened a store in 1974 that offered an alternative to the traditional grocery store. The store's proud manager and some delighted customers are pictured at the opening of the store in Christmas week.

*Above:* Between 1880 and 1905, Joseph Lovell ran a butcher's shop at No. 5 Brook Street. He was one of nine town centre butchers in business at the turn of the century. The staff are posing in front of an attractive display of items for sale in around 1900.

*Below:* One of the most prestigious businesses was the drapery emporium run by Richard Northcott Stranger in Manchester House in Pym Street. On this day, around 1913, the shop is closed for the staff outing.

The Bedford Hotel has been Tavistock's principal hostelry since the building was converted from the private residence of the Duke of Bedford's steward in 1822. It is seen here in 1880.

The Queen's Head Hotel in 1996, looking forlorn and forgotten. It had just closed its doors for the last time after a long lifetime as a town centre hostelry. Its heyday had been the coaching era. After a long period of neglect, it was completely renovated and greeted the twenty-first century as Brown's Restaurant.

The Doidge family, seen here in the 1920s, were the last tenants of the Temperance Hotel in Pym Street, which was built in 1838. The building subsequently went through a series of conversions and changes of function, emerging at the end as the Ordulph Arms.

Bill Foster outside his popular Pym Street bakery in 2001, the year in which he retired and moved to France. Bill the Baker was an institution in the town.

*Above:* Children competing: The formidable Mrs Roberts supervises the annual gala at the town's open-air swimming pool above Bannawell Street, a gift from the ninth Duke of Bedford in 1883. The pool, which provided facilities for competition and recreation, closed in 1989 and was superseded by the Meadowlands pool.

*Left:* Dogs competing: One of the annual dog shows in the Pannier Market in the 1960s. Flair and his owner Mrs Morris are impressing Judge Atkinson during the judging of the Cavalier King Charles Spaniel Class.

Flowers competing: George Knott (right) lived the whole of his life from 1903 to 1972 in Tavistock. A quarryman, he lost a leg in an accident. He was for many years associated with the Gardening Club, and was the secretary of its Spring Flower Show. He is seen here having a discussion with Judge Merrifield during one of the flower shows.

Vegetables competing: Local horticultural shows had for many years a regular contributor, and winner, in Tom Smale. A well-known and popular figure, he was a First World War veteran who lived into his nineties, and into the nineties of the twentieth century, in his Sunshine Terrace home.

If you are interested in purchasing other books published by The History Press, or in case you have difficulty finding any of our books in your local bookshop, you can also place orders directly through our website

**www.thehistorypress.co.uk**